Layman's Bible Book Commentary
Matthew

LAYMAN'S BIBLE BOOK COMMENTARY

LBBC

MATTHEW

VOLUME 15

Clair M. Crissey

BROADMAN PRESS
Nashville, Tennessee

© Copyright 1981 • Broadman Press

All rights reserved.

4211-85

ISBN: 0-8054-1185-2

Dewey Decimal Classification: 226.2

Subject heading: BIBLE. N. T. MATTHEW

Library of Congress Catalog Card Number: 79-56691

Printed in the United States of America

Foreword

The *Layman's Bible Book Commentary* in twenty-four volumes was planned as a practical exposition of the whole Bible for lay readers and students. It is based on the conviction that the Bible speaks to every generation of believers but needs occasional reinterpretation in the light of changing language and modern experience. Following the guidance of God's Spirit, the believer finds in it the authoritative word for faith and life.

To meet the needs of lay readers, the *Commentary* is written in a popular style, and each Bible book is clearly outlined to reveal its major emphases. Although the writers are competent scholars and reverent interpreters, they have avoided critical problems and the use of original languages except where they were essential for explaining the text. They recognize the variety of literary forms in the Bible, but they have not followed documentary trails or become preoccupied with literary concerns. Their primary purpose was to show what each Bible book meant for its time and what it says to our own generation.

The Revised Standard Version of the Bible is the basic text of the *Commentary*, but writers were free to use other translations to clarify an occasional passage or sharpen its effect. To provide as much interpretation as possible in such concise books, the Bible text was not printed along with the comment.

Of the twenty-four volumes of the *Commentary*, fourteen deal with Old Testament books and ten with those in the New Testament. The volumes range in pages from 140 to 168. Four major books in the Old Testament and five in the New are treated in one volume each. Others appear in various combinations. Although the allotted space varies, each Bible book is treated as a whole to reveal its basic message with some passages getting special attention. Whatever plan of Bible study the reader may follow, this *Commentary* will be a valuable companion.

Despite the best-seller reputation of the Bible, the average survey of Bible knowledge reveals a good deal of ignorance about it and its primary meaning. Many adult church members seem to think that its study is intended for children and preachers. But some of the newer translations have been making the Bible more readable for all ages. Bible study has branched out from Sunday into other days of the week, and into neighborhoods rather than just in churches. This *Commentary* wants to meet the growing need for insight into all that the Bible has to say about God and his world and about Christ and his fellowship.

BROADMAN PRESS

Unless otherwise marked, Scripture quotations are from the Revised Standard Version of the Bible; copyrighted 1946, 1952, © 1971, 1973.

Verses marked KJV are from the King James Version of the Bible.

Contents

Introduction

The Gospel of Matthew

The Gospel of Matthew has likely influenced more people than any other Christian book. This role of influence probably began for Matthew's Gospel with its acceptance by Antioch, a great early Christian center.

Our four New Testament Gospels were all completed and brought together by sometime in the second century AD. Matthew's Gospel was placed first among them. Since that time Matthew has remained the most popular of the four Gospel accounts. Even those Christians whose favorite Gospel is Mark, Luke, or John probably use Matthew more than the others. The greater use of Matthew comes in part from its first-place position in the printed New Testament. Also, only Matthew's Gospel contains the Sermon on the Mount.

Each of the Gospels is different, but the differences between them do not mean the accounts are unreliable. Instead, the differences show that God used different individuals who had varying purposes and perspectives to give us a far richer view of Christ than one Gospel alone could ever give.

About This Gospel's Author

Late in the first century AD, a Christian teacher set this account of Jesus' life and teachings down in writing. Early tradition attributed this writing to Matthew, one of Jesus' twelve apostles. A statement made by a Christian bishop in the second century AD is the basis for this tradition.

Many Bible scholars today doubt that Matthew wrote all of this Gospel. They point out the fact that an eyewitness to the events described would not have needed to use Mark's Gospel as a major source, as this Gospel's author did. They also feel sure that this Gospel was originally written in Greek, not in Hebrew, as the early tradition held.

Yet it seems certain that Matthew was connected in some way

with the writing of this Gospel which bears his name. At the very least, he may have been the compiler of the sayings of Jesus used in this Gospel or the collector of the large number of Old Testament Scriptures and prophecies also used in it.

What do we know about the apostle Matthew? He was a tax collector working near Capernaum under Herod Antipas' authority. Jesus called Matthew, also known as Levi, to be his follower as Matthew sat in the tax office (see Matt. 9:9-13; Mark 2:13-17; Luke 5:27-32). After he had followed Jesus, Matthew invited Jesus to a feast at his home. Other tax collectors and "sinners" were also present at this meal (see Luke 5:29-30).

Matthew's Gospel does show the kind of interest in precise organization we would expect of a tax collector. It also reveals an interest in money. For instance, two of Jesus' parables which involve money are found only in this Gospel. They are the parable of the unmerciful servant (18:23-35) and the parable of the vineyard laborers (20:1-16).

The author of this Gospel chose to stress Christ, not himself, in his writing. The value of the writing lies in its influence on countless readers over the centuries, not in certainty about its author's identity.

This Gospel's Purposes and Distinctives

Purposes.—A study of Matthew's Gospel reveals several probable purposes behind its writing.

No doubt the author's main purpose in writing was to convince his fellow Jews that Jesus was indeed the expected Messiah. This Gospel gives special emphasis to Jesus' fulfillment of God's redemptive purposes shown in the Old Testament.

Another of the author's purposes was to present and stress Jesus' teachings. Mark's Gospel had vividly presented the story of Jesus' ministry but had omitted many of his teachings. This Gospel, then, combined the narrative of events with a fuller account of the teachings.

The author of Matthew's Gospel was also likely trying to answer the accusations which critics had brought about Jesus. His record of Jesus' birth, for example, would have answered those who were saying that Jesus' birth had been illegitimate. His inclusion of the story of Joseph's and Mary's flight to Egypt and return to live in Nazareth would have explained why Jesus had grown up in Nazareth instead of Bethlehem (where the Messiah was expected to live). And his account of the bribing of the soldiers at Jesus' tomb would have answered those who were charging that Jesus' body had been stolen.

It is probable that the writer was organizing all available material into a form usable for teaching or worship. This Gospel is well suited for both purposes.

Distinctives.—Matthew's Gospel has several distinctive characteristics.

The first of these characteristics is the author's conciseness. He often used narratives based on Mark's account. But in most instances he condensed them so that he would have more room to include related teachings of Jesus.

Matthew's Gospel alone of the four New Testament Gospels makes specific mention of the church. These references are found in Matthew 16:18 and 18:17.

Matthew also stressed "last things," the coming of the end time. His parables of the ten maidens, the talents, and the sheep and the goats are found in this Gospel alone.

Finally, this Gospel, more than the others, includes quotations from the Old Testament. In fact, the author included almost seventy of these quotations from sixteen Old Testament books. These quotations helped the writer prove to his readers that Jesus was the Messiah, the fulfillment of the Law and the Prophets.

Date, Place of Writing, Destination

Most Bible scholars believe that Matthew's Gospel was written about AD 80-90. No one can be sure where it was written, but Palestine is a likely place for its origin. It seems that its original intended readers were Jewish, since the writer expected them to be familiar with the Jewish customs he mentioned without explaining.

Sources Used in the Gospel's Writing

Inspired by the Holy Spirit, the writer of Matthew's Gospel skillfully wove together the materials available to him. What were these sources?

1) *Mark's Gospel*—The major organizational framework of

Matthew's Gospel came from Mark's account. However, the author of Matthew's Gospel condensed much of Mark's narrative and added a great deal of new material.

2) *A sayings source*—A little more than half of the material in Matthew's Gospel not found in Mark's Gospel is repeated in Luke's Gospel. So it seems that the author of both Matthew's and Luke's Gospels used a common source for this material.

3) *A source special to Matthew*—The author was familiar with stories about and teachings of Jesus found in neither Mark's Gospel nor in the sayings source he shared with Luke.

4) *A collection of Old Testament quotations*—As stated earlier, the author of Matthew's Gospel made extensive use of Old Testament references. He may have been using an already existing collection of quotations interpreted as referring to Jesus.

The Structure of Matthew's Gospel

The author of Matthew's Gospel carefully arranged his material in a form which could be used by the church for teaching. He began by telling the story of Jesus' birth and infancy (chapters 1 and 2). He ended his Gospel with the story of Jesus' crucifixion and resurrection (chapters 26—28).

In between, the author grouped his material around five great discourses of Jesus, alternating narrative material with Jesus' teachings. He made each of the five sections conclude with a statement similar to that found at the end of the first discourse: "And when Jesus finished these sayings . . ." (7:28; the other concluding statements are in 11:1; 13:53; 19:1; and 26:1).

This Gospel's Meaning for Today

Today, as throughout the Christian centuries, Matthew's Gospel speaks to human spiritual needs. It presents the One whose demands are higher than those of any written law. Yet it also reveals him as the Savior whose divine love for us led him to the cross.

Matthew's Gospel makes clear for all time the truth that in Jesus God's purposes have found fulfillment. This full and orderly account of the gospel, the good news about Jesus, still calls, instructs, and inspires those who are willing to hear and follow him.

Beginnings
1:1 to 4:25

The Genealogy of Jesus (1:1-17)

Most people simply skip over the genealogies of the Bible. After all, lists of obscure, long-dead people aren't very interesting, are they? But, as you will see, Matthew had a definite purpose in starting his Gospel with Jesus' genealogy. And there is far more to this genealogy than is apparent at first glance.

In the very first verse of his Gospel, Matthew used the title "Jesus Christ." Even the name has much significance. The Hebrew equivalent of Jesus is "Joshua," which means "The Lord is salvation." You may recall that God had called Joshua to lead his people into the Promised Land. In a similar way, Jesus was the Savior who would lead people out of sin and into God's kingdom. "Christ" is the Greek equivalent of the Hebrew word for Messiah. Messiah means "the Anointed One."

The Jews set great store by family pedigrees. They would not believe in Jesus as Messiah unless they could see his descent from Abraham and David. Matthew was intent on showing that Jesus was both "son of David" and "son of Abraham" (v. 1).

It was to Abraham that God had first given his promise of blessing for all nations (see Gen. 12:3). None of Abraham's descendants had fulfilled this prophecy. And to David, God had promised an everlasting kingdom (see 2 Sam. 7:12-13). Yet none of David's descendants had fulfilled that prophecy, either. Matthew was saying that in Jesus Christ the promises given to Abraham and to David had come to fulfillment.

Matthew divided the genealogy itself into three sections, each covering one phase of Jewish history. The first section goes from Abraham to David, the greatest king of Israel. This was the time of Israel's rise to glory (vv. 2-6). The second section covers Jewish history from the time of David's son Solomon to the Babylonian exile. Shame and failure marked this period of Hebrew history (vv. 7-11). The third section includes the time up until the coming of Jesus, the Savior of all people (vv. 12-16).

The genealogy given us by Matthew has several points of special interest. For instance, contrary to Jewish custom, Matthew included four women in his genealogy. Moreover, these were not women one might expect to be included. Tamar was an adulteress (v. 3). Ruth, a Moabitess, was not a Jew (v. 5). Rahab was a harlot (v. 5). And Bathsheba, the wife of Uriah, had been wrongfully taken by David (v. 6).

But the inclusion of these four women shows that God can use all kinds of people, even very imperfect ones, in the carrying out of his plan. His love is universal. Something more can be seen here— a foreshadowing of the barriers Jesus would remove. In him, barriers between Jew and Gentile, male and female, and the righteous and the unrighteous would be broken down.

Note that Matthew, in this case true to Jewish custom, traced Jesus' descent through Joseph, though Joseph was not Jesus' real father. According to Jewish law, however, Joseph, as Mary's husband, was Jesus' legal father. And being Joseph's legal son gave Jesus the same status he would have had as his actual son.

This introductory portion of Matthew's Gospel, then, presents an important truth: Jesus is the Messiah from the line of David, the fulfillment of the promises God made to Abraham and to David. This passage also provides some insight into the kind of Savior Jesus was to be.

The Birth of the Messiah (1:18-25)

Matthew's description of circumstances surrounding Jesus' birth focused attention on Joseph, the husband of Mary. In contrast, Luke, in his Gospel, told the story from the point of view of Jesus' mother, Mary.

After Mary and Joseph were betrothed but "before they came together" (v. 18), Joseph learned that Mary was pregnant. During the year of betrothal, a couple was considered husband and wife but did not live together. Joseph could think only that Mary was guilty of adultery, which could even be punished by stoning. He was a good man. In spite of the sin he believed she had committed, Joseph did not want to expose Mary to public shame and danger. For that reason, he decided to take advantage of a provision of the law which would permit him to divorce her privately.

At that point, God intervened in Joseph's plans. In a dream, an angel of God told Joseph that Mary's child had been conceived "of the Holy Spirit" (v. 20). Joseph shouldn't hesitate to go ahead and marry Mary, making her son legitimately his.

In those days, fathers named their children. The angel told Joseph that he should name Mary's son *Jesus.* Names had more importance in Bible times than they have today. Often a person's name described or characterized him. The name "Jesus" described one who would, as the angel told Joseph, "save his people from their sins" (v. 21).

The Jewish people wanted and expected a Messiah who would save them from the rule of Rome. Jesus would save them from the even more devastating rule of sin.

Matthew saw in the coming of Jesus the complete fulfillment of Isaiah 7:14 (v. 22). That prophecy had called the son who would be born "Emmanuel," meaning "God with us" (v. 23). Jesus would be not merely a man acting for God, but God himself dwelling among his people.

Matthew wrote that Joseph was fully convinced by the angel's words. He married Mary. And when her son was born, he called the child Jesus.

Visitors from Afar (2:1-12)

In chapter 2, verse 1, Matthew provided information about the place and general time of Jesus' birth. Jesus' birth took place in Bethlehem, just a few miles south of Jerusalem. Bethlehem had also been David's city. Jesus' birth took place in the time when Herod was king. This Herod was Herod the Great, who ruled from 40—4 BC.

Matthew went on to tell of an unusual event which occurred close to the time of Jesus' birth. The Wise Men, or Magi, came from the East to Jerusalem, looking for the newborn Jewish king. These were men who studied the heavens. They had seen a new star which they interpreted as heralding the birth of the long-hoped-for Messiah of the Jews. They had traveled from their home in the East to pay homage to this king.

Herod heard about the Magi's search for the Jewish king and was deeply troubled. He was only part-Jewish and was very jealous of any threat to his throne. The whole city of Jerusalem was troubled, too, since Herod's cruelties were well known where rivals to his power were concerned. Herod had had one of his wives and her mother killed. He had also had some of his own sons executed.

Understandably, Herod was anxious to locate this newborn threat to his throne. He called in the chief priests and scribes to learn where, according to Scripture, the Messiah would be born. These religious authorities quoted Micah 5:2. Bethlehem was to be the Messiah's birthplace (vv. 4-6).

Herod called the Wise Men to him and found out from them when they had seen the unusual star appear. Then he sent them on their way to Bethlehem, with instructions to return to him once they had found the baby king. Herod deceitfully claimed that he, too, wanted to worship the Messiah.

The Wise Men went on their way. This time they saw the star again and followed it to the place where Jesus was. By now, Jesus, Mary, and Joseph were staying in a house, rather than in the stable where, according to Luke, Jesus had been born.

The Wise Men paid homage to Jesus and opened the gifts they had brought him. There was gold, the symbol of kingship. There was frankincense, associated with holiness and worship. And there was myrrh, which was used in embalming the dead. While Jesus was still a baby, these gifts foretold his roles as king, priest, and one who would suffer and die.

In a dream, God warned the Magi not to go back to Herod in Jerusalem. So they returned, by another route, to their own country.

Why was this story important to Matthew? It showed that Gentiles, foreigners, were receptive to Jesus even from the time of his birth. This openness stood in sharp contrast to the indifference and rejection Jesus faced from his own people. The religious leaders, when told of his birth, had done nothing to find him. This story also showed that the powers of the earth, represented by Herod, stood opposed to Jesus from the very beginning.

Escape from Herod (2:13-18)

Danger awaited Jesus, for Herod planned to find and kill him. But God intervened to save his Son. Again, Joseph had a dream. This time an angel warned him to leave Bethlehem quickly, taking Jesus and Mary with him. They were to flee to Egypt, a Roman province not under Herod's rule. Joseph obeyed at once.

In Moses' day, Egypt had been a place of oppression for God's people. Now, as earlier in the days of Abraham and Jacob, it was to be a refuge. A great many Jews lived in Egypt, and it is probable that Mary and Joseph found a haven among them. Could it be that they paid for this journey to and stay in Egypt with the gifts of the Wise Men?

Matthew wrote that Jesus' family remained in Egypt until Herod died (4 BC). He saw in this fact a fulfillment of some words from Hosea 11:1 (v. 15). Originally, Hosea had been speaking of God's freeing of his people from Egyptian bondage. Matthew looked deeper and saw Jesus repeating the experience of the Israelites by being called out of Egypt.

But Herod had not taken lightly the failure of the Wise Men to return to him. He had ordered all the male children of Bethlehem two years of age or less to be killed. Of course, he hoped the messianic king-to-be was among those he had had murdered.

Again, Matthew saw Scripture fulfilled (vv. 17-18). The sorrow over the slain babies of Bethlehem was like that described by Jeremiah. Jeremiah had spoken of Rachel, the mother of Benjamin and Joseph, weeping as residents of Jerusalem were marched past her tomb, not far from Bethlehem, to captivity in Babylon (see Jer. 31:15).

To Nazareth (2:19-23)

After Herod the Great had died and the danger to Jesus was past, God once again gave Joseph instructions in a dream. Joseph, Mary, and Jesus were to return to Israel. As before, Joseph obeyed without questioning.

On returning to Israel, however, Joseph learned that Archelaus, an especially cruel son of Herod the Great, was ruling Judea. A dream again instructed Joseph, telling him to go to Galilee. Galilee was ruled by Herod Antipas, who remained ruler there during all of Jesus' life.

Matthew noted that within Galilee, Joseph and his family went to live in the city of Nazareth. According to Luke, Nazareth had been Mary's and Joseph's home before Jesus' birth in Bethlehem (see Luke

1:26-27; 2:4). Matthew called the fact of Jesus' residence in Nazareth a fulfillment of the prophets' words that the Messiah would be
known as a Nazarene (v. 23).

Matthew's statement is somewhat difficult to interpret, since no
reference to Nazareth can be found in the Old Testament. One
explanation, however, may shed some light on Matthew's possible
meaning. Isaiah had prophesied that men would despise the Servant
of the Lord. Some of the contempt shown for Jesus can be seen in the
words of Nathanael who, when told about Jesus asked, "Can anything good come out of Nazareth?" (John 1:46). Perhaps Matthew
was not quoting a prophecy word for word but was saying that Jesus'
residence in Nazareth caused people to show contempt for him, as
Isaiah had prophesied.

The Mission of John the Baptist (3:1-6)

Matthew remained silent about the events of the thirty or so years
after Jesus' family settled in Nazareth. He resumed his story with
the sudden appearance of John the Baptist in Judea's wilderness.

John's preaching called for the people to repent and announced
the nearness of the "kingdom of heaven" (v. 2). The phrase "kingdom of heaven" has the same meaning as "kingdom of God." That
meaning is God's kingly rule. Of course, God has always been sov-
ereign ruler of the world, though not all people have acknowledged
him as such. But John was proclaiming the fact that God was about
to make his rule known in a special way.

Matthew saw John the Baptist as the fulfillment of Isaiah 40:1-5
(v. 3). That passage spoke of God's coming to lead his people out of
their exile in Babylon. It mentioned a voice which cried out for a
way to be made straight for the coming of God. Matthew saw John
the Baptist as that voice preparing the hearts of the people for the
coming of the Messiah, who would lead them out of sin's exile.

John's clothing reminded the people of the ancient prophet Elijah
(see 2 Kings 1:8). (It was generally believed that Elijah would return
just before the Messiah made his appearance.) John wore camel's
hair clothing with a leather girdle. He lived off the land, eating in-
sects (locusts) and wild honey (v. 4).

The appearance of so striking a prophet, after centuries without a
prophet, brought out large crowds from all the surrounding region.

John baptized these people in the Jordan River. There is no question about the fact that he immersed them. The word used for baptized means "dipped." More important, the people repented, confessing their sins. Repentance means a turning from sin, a submission of one's life to God's rule.

The unusual fact about John's preaching and baptism was that he called Jews to baptism and repentance. The Jews believed that the Gentiles needed to repent and be baptized. But it was a new thing to make these demands of Jews.

Confrontation with the Pharisees and Sadducees (3:7-12)

Even some Pharisees and Sadducees, Jewish religious leaders, came asking John for baptism. Their request brought an angry verbal attack from John. He called them a "brood of vipers" fleeing "from the wrath to come" (v. 7). John meant they were like snakes fleeing for their lives from a desert fire or from the harvester's sickle. Fear, not true repentance, was their only motive in coming.

Verbal repentance wasn't enough. These men had to "bear fruit" (v. 8), meaning they must live lives which would show their repentance was genuine, that they had changed direction.

The Pharisees were the most religious laymen of their day. They wanted to keep God's law. But they had made more and more rules and had come to think of themselves as the only ones who were righteous.

The Sadducees were in charge of the Temple and the religious government of the Jews. But they could keep their power only as they cooperated with the pagan Roman authorities. They seem to have believed only in the first five books of the Old Testament as Scripture. And they were generally worldly and materialistic.

John knew that the Pharisees and Sadducees, along with other Jews, believed that Abraham's righteousness was enough to save them from judgment in the life to come. After all, they were Abraham's descendants. But John the Baptist insisted that they could take no refuge in the fact that Abraham was their ancestor. Judgment would be on an individual basis.

John used the analogy of trees to describe the Jews. Already the woodman held his axe ready to cut down any tree which did not give a yield of good fruit. The cut trees would be burned (v. 10).

John described his baptism as one "for repentance" (v. 11). But he looked ahead to the One who was coming after him. At that time, John was enjoying popularity and influence. Yet he declared that he was not even fit to perform a slave's duties for the mightier One who was to come.

That One would have a different kind of baptism to give. He would baptize "with the Holy Spirit and with fire" (v. 11). Salvation and judgment would be the two sides to his work. He would bring the Holy Spirit into people's lives, enabling them to direct their lives toward God. But he would also bring the fire of judgment.

John used the symbolism of the threshing floor to describe the Messiah's judgment (v. 12). In that time (as in some places today) animals trod out the grain, leaving the grain and chaff mixed together on the threshing floor. With the winnowing fork, the mixture was thrown into the air. Most of the chaff blew away, but the grain remained. The grain was then stored, while any remaining chaff was burned. In a similar way, the Messiah would cause a separation to be made between those who would repent and receive him and those who would not.

The Baptism of Jesus (3:13-17)

Word of John's appearance and preaching reached the city of Nazareth where Jesus lived. The year must have been about AD 26. Jesus had, no doubt, been waiting for the right time to begin his ministry. The coming of John indicated to Jesus that his hour had finally arrived. John had made people realize their sin and their need for repentance. The forerunner's work was complete.

So Jesus made the trip from his home in Galilee to the Jordan River. There he presented himself to John for baptism. We do not know whether Jesus and John were acquainted before this meeting at the Jordan. We do know, from Luke's Gospel, that Jesus' mother and John's mother were related (see Luke 1:36). But John recognized the fact that Jesus alone had no need of his baptism. John admitted his own unworthiness at once, declaring that he had need of being baptized by Jesus, instead.

Jesus, however, insisted that John baptize him. His reason was that he needed "to fulfil all righteousness" (v. 15). He meant that by being baptized he would be doing God's will.

We know that Jesus had no sin of his own, so he did not need a baptism symbolizing repentance. Why, then, did Jesus feel his baptism was necessary? In being baptized by John, he first showed that he was in agreement with John's ministry with its call to a new relationship to God. Jesus also was identifying with those he had come to save from sin. Finally, his baptism looked ahead to the salvation he would bring to mankind. Jesus' immersion in the water and his rising up from it provided a symbolic forecast of his death, burial, and resurrection.

As Jesus was raised from the water, a remarkable thing happened. Jesus saw the opening of the heavens. And God's Spirit descended "like a dove" (v. 16). Then God the Father spoke some significant words. He declared Jesus to be his "beloved Son, with whom" he was "well pleased" (v. 17).

These words of God have a meaning far deeper than what appears on the surface. You see, God spoke to his Son in words of Scripture. This statement is, in fact, made up of two quotations from the Old Testament. The first Old Testament passage, Psalm 2:7, spoke in context of God's crowning of the Messiah King. The second, Isaiah 42:1, came from a chapter which spoke of God's ideal Servant. Jesus, then, was to be the Messiah King for whom the people had been waiting. But he would not be a conquering military hero. Instead he would be the obedient Servant of the Lord.

In this scene at the Jordan, the Trinity was clearly present. Jesus, the Son, was ordained and equipped there for his messianic ministry. The Holy Spirit came to anoint and empower him. And God the Father spoke his approval of the Son as Jesus set out on the mission to which he had now dedicated himself.

Temptations in the Wilderness (4:1-11)

After Jesus' baptism, the Spirit led him into an uninhabited wilderness area. There Jesus was to face temptation by the devil. A temptation is actually a testing for the purpose of proving. The devil hoped to prove Jesus unfaithful to his Father.

It is impossible to fully understand these temptations without first understanding the baptism which preceded them. At his baptism Jesus had been assured of his destiny as Messiah and had been equipped for it by the Spirit. But he had been called to fulfill that

destiny by following the path of being God's Servant. The temptations Jesus underwent in the wilderness were attempts to make him
so aware of his role and powers as Messiah that he would avoid the
difficult way God had laid out for him.

Only the Messiah could have faced these particular temptations.
We know from Hebrews 2:18 that Jesus faced the kinds of temptations we face. But these wilderness temptations were part of Jesus'
inner struggle as he tried to decide what kind of Messiah he would be
and how he would win people for God.

This struggle was an inward, spiritual, and no doubt agonizing
one. Jesus himself must later have described it to his followers in a
way they could understand.

To win the world with bread (4:2-4).—The first temptation Jesus
faced was a twofold one. He had spent forty days and nights fasting
in the wilderness. At the end of that time he must have been very
hungry. The devil used that hunger to suggest a way for Jesus to use
his powers.

There were stones on the ground which may have resembled small
loaves of bread. The devil told Jesus to use his power to "command
these stones to become loaves of bread" (v. 3).

He preceded that suggestion and the next one with the phrase "If
you are the Son of God . . ." He was not expressing doubt or trying
to get Jesus to prove his Sonship. In Greek, the phrase assumed Jesus
was God's Son and meant "Since you are God's Son."

What did this first temptation mean to Jesus? First of all, the devil
was suggesting that Jesus use his power to satisfy his own hunger.
But, more than that, he was reminding Jesus of the hunger of others.
What better way to win the world than by providing food for all?
Jesus, however, realized that in spite of his compassion for needy
people, he must not try to win them with food or other material
things. That would be a form of bribery. And people would be following him solely for the things he could give them. He had come to
call people to give rather than get.

Jesus realized, too, that hunger was not the people's main problem. Hunger was just one of the many symptoms of the disease of sin.
For sin, in such forms as selfishness and ruthlessness, caused material
need for many. Jesus knew that God was the real and most basic

need of the people. He had to proclaim God's Word to them and satisfy the hunger of their hearts. So he answered Satan with words from Scripture, quoting Deuteronomy 8:3 (v. 4).

To win the world with amazing feats (4:5-7).—Having failed the first time, the devil tried again. Possibly in a vision, he took Jesus to the highest portion of the Temple and told Jesus to throw himself off. He quoted Psalm 91:11-12 to Jesus. That Scripture promised God's protection for those who put their trust in him (v. 6).

Satan was suggesting that Jesus draw followers by performing amazing feats. Surely God would not allow his Son to die or be harmed in a plunge from the Temple. People wanted to see miracles, and Jesus could use the certainty of God's protection to win huge crowds.

But Jesus realized that such an act would be tempting God. God expected his followers to take risks in order to do his will. But to deliberately place oneself in danger to force God's protection would be testing God. Jesus quoted Deuteronomy 6:16 to answer Satan (v. 7).

Notice that the devil quoted Scripture. Scripture, then, can be used in right or wrong ways, for good or for evil purposes. The mere fact that someone quotes Scripture does not mean he is doing God's will. Neither does it mean that he understands Scripture.

Later Jesus did work many miracles. But he never worked miracles to get followers or to cause people to believe in him. His miraculous works came from his compassion for the people and as signs that in him God was at work.

To win the world with Satan's methods (4:8-10).—Satan tried yet a third time. Probably in a vision, he showed Jesus "all the kingdoms of the world" (v. 8). He proposed to give all this to Jesus, if Jesus would only bow down and worship him (v. 9).

Here Satan was trying to persuade Jesus to win the world with his diabolical methods. The people wanted a military Messiah, didn't they? They wanted freedom from Rome. So why not use force to win the world? Satan was saying that the good result (dominion over the world) would justify the ruthless means which would have to be used.

Jesus once again answered Satan with Scripture. Quoting Deuteronomy 6:13, he declared that only God deserved worship and service (v. 10). To win the world by force would be to worship Satan instead of God.

Jesus could have won the whole world if he had been willing to use Satan's weapons. But God had called him to the way of service and self-sacrifice. Any who chose to follow him must do so of their own free will.

The devil's departure (4:11).—The devil then left, though only temporarily. His attempts to sway Jesus had been failures. Of course, Jesus faced these and other temptations again and again throughout his ministry. But the first battle was won.

God's people, the ancient Israelites, had faced testing in the wilderness and had proved unfaithful. In contrast to them, Jesus proved faithful. Adam, the first man, had given in to Satan's testing, wanting to be like God himself. But Jesus, who was God's Son, chose the way of service to his Father, wherever that way might lead.

Ministry in Galilee (4:12-17)

Upon hearing that John the Baptist had been put in prison, Jesus returned to Galilee. Galilee was heavily populated and would offer a wide audience for his message. But Jesus left his hometown of Nazareth and instead made Capernaum the headquarters for his ministry in Galilee. Capernaum was one of the cities on the northern shore of the Sea of Galilee.

Matthew looked at Jesus' choice of Galilee for his place of initial ministry as the fulfillment of Isaiah 9:1-2. The Assyrians had overtaken Galilee (formerly known as Zebulun and Naphtali) in the eighth century BC. From then on the land was paganized, though the Maccabees in the second century BC forcibly "converted" to Judaism many of the Gentiles there. Isaiah had prophesied the coming of a descendant of David, one who would bring light to this darkened region. Matthew saw Jesus as that Light which had come to shine on Galilee (vv. 14-16).

After moving to Capernaum, Jesus began preaching. His first message was identical to that of John the Baptist. He called on people to repent because of the nearness of God's kingdom. The message was the same; Jesus himself made the difference. In him the kingdom of God had stopped being in the future and had become present tense.

First Disciples (4:18-22)

Jesus wanted more than a ministry of teaching and preaching. He also needed a close group of followers who could share in his work. So very early in his ministry, Jesus called four men to be his disciples. He called these first disciples from their work as fishermen on the Sea of Galilee.

Jesus saw the first two, brothers named Andrew and Simon Peter, as they were casting nets. We know from John's Gospel that Jesus had already become acquainted with these two during the ministry of John the Baptist (see John 1:40-42).

Now he called them to a decisive following. From that time on, he told them, he would make them "fishers of men" (v. 19). They would be using God's nets to draw people up from sin. Matthew wrote that Peter and Andrew "immediately" followed Jesus, leaving their nets behind (v. 20).

Next, two other brothers received Jesus' call. They too were fishermen and may have also known Jesus earlier. When Jesus came upon them, James and John were mending nets in their boat with their father, Zebedee. At Jesus' call, James and John left not only the boat but also their father and followed him.

Teaching, Preaching, and Healing (4:23-25)

In verses 23-25, Matthew provided a brief overview of the kind of ministry Jesus carried out in Galilee. Following chapters of his Gospel describe this ministry in greater detail.

It seems that Jesus confined his early work to Galilee. It was a threefold ministry—teaching, preaching, and healing (v. 23).

Much of Jesus' teaching must have taken place in the synagogues of Galilee. No better place could have been found for getting new religious concepts across. Synagogues had become important as places of worship and study during the Exile, when the Jews had been separated from their Temple. And the synagogues continued to be important even after the Temple was restored.

The Jewish people met in their synagogues on the sabbath for prayer, readings from the Scripture, and an address often given by a visitor. Jesus' teaching in the synagogues may have consisted of his interpretation of the portions of Scripture which had been read.

In addition to teaching, Jesus had a preaching ministry. He proclaimed "the gospel of the kingdom" (v. 23). It was good news (the gospel) that God was breaking into human history in a new and different way.

Jesus then translated his spoken proclamation of God's reign into action by healing the many diseases and infirmities of the people. His healing showed that God's kingly power to overcome evil was present in him. He healed multitudes who had all kinds of afflictions.

Not surprisingly, news of Jesus' ministry spread widely. From Syria in the north and Judea to the south, from the Decapolis (the ten Greek cities mostly east of the Jordan River), and from "beyond the Jordan" (v. 25), huge crowds followed to hear him and to be healed by him.

The Sermon on the Mount
5:1 to 7:29

The Setting (5:1-2)

Matthew wrote that "seeing the crowds," Jesus went up on a mountain to teach (v. 1). There "he sat down" and his followers, the disciples, came close to hear him (v. 1). No doubt the rest of the crowd listened as well.

It seems likely that in this scene Matthew saw Jesus as a second Moses giving God's new law to the people. The mountain, probably a hill near the Sea of Galilee, would have reminded Matthew of Mount Sinai, from which Moses had spoken.

The Way to Blessedness (5:3-12)

Jesus first presented his hearers with nine Beatitudes. These Beatitudes instructed those who would follow Jesus in how to have real and lasting happiness. In each, "blessed are" could be translated "happy are."

"The poor in spirit" (5:3).—Jesus declared that "the poor in spirit" are happy because "the kingdom of heaven" is theirs. These people are those who realize their own spiritual poverty. They know that they themselves lack the power to do what God wants them to do. They put all their trust in God's ability to supply their spiritual need.

The poor in spirit may also be poor in terms of earthly riches. Recognizing that wealth doesn't bring lasting happiness, they choose to be ruled by God rather than by the pursuit of material things. The kingdom of heaven belongs to those who realize that their primary need is their need of God.

"Those who mourn" (5:4).—Jesus promised that "those who mourn" will ultimately be comforted. Those who feel sorrowful because of their own sins and failure and because of the world's evil which leads to so much suffering will some day know God's comfort. The reasons for mourning will be gone when God's rule over all things is complete.

"The meek" (5:5).—Jesus promised inheritance of the earth (or the land) to the meek. The word "meek" has come to be equated with words like "weak" or "spineless." But this is not the meaning Jesus had in mind. The meek person is one whose trust is in God rather than in himself. This person sees his or her limitations and so puts dependence on God.

Psalm 37:11 declared that "the meek shall possess the land." God had given a Promised Land to his people in the Old Testament. He had yet a new future "land" to give to those who would be part of his kingdom. On earth now, the violent and tyrannical often have possession. But the new land of promise will be inherited by those whose trust is in the greatness of God.

"Those who hunger and thirst for righteousness" (5:6).—Jesus said that those who hunger and thirst for righteousness will be satisfied. These people are those who want, more than anything else, to see the world's evil (including what is wrong in their own lives) overcome by God's righteousness. (This yearning would have to include a willingness to do what is right themselves.) They want this righteousness as much as a starving person wants food and as much as a person dying of thirst wants water. Jesus promised these people that God's righteousness would finally prevail, and their desire for it would be satisfied.

"The merciful" (5:7).—Jesus next taught that the merciful would themselves "obtain mercy" (v. 7). Merciful people realize their own unworthiness and need for God's pardon. Having known God's grace and pardon in their own lives, they want to forgive and help others.

God does not show mercy to the merciful as a reward. To be merciful is the nature of God. But merciful people, those who can give mercy and forgiveness to others, are themselves the people who are open to receiving forgiveness themselves. Those who cannot forgive others are not open to receiving forgiveness for themselves.

The presence of mercy in people's lives shows that they are children of God. The merciful can know that God will show mercy to them even as they have shown it to others.

"The pure in heart" (5:8).—Jesus promised that "the pure in heart" would "see God" (v. 8). The pure in heart are those who serve God with single-minded devotion and unmixed motives. The "heart" means the inner self, including a person's mind.

Some Jews in Jesus' day put a great deal of emphasis on outward, ritual purity. Here Jesus stressed the more important purity of the inner life in its relationship to God. But this inner condition would express itself in the outward life the "pure in heart" would live. God cannot remain unseen by the person whose life is lived in whole-hearted devotion to him.

"The peacemakers" (5:9).—Jesus declared that peacemakers would "be called sons of God" (v. 9). He promised this blessing not to those who are neutral or to those who merely love peace but to those who are actively involved in making peace.

Christ himself was the " 'Prince of Peace' " (Isa. 9:6). He came to bring reconciliation between God and mankind and between individuals. Those who, through him, are at peace with God, can join him in his work of reconciliation. They will then be called God's sons because, as peacemakers, they will share in God's nature and character.

"Those who are persecuted for righteousness' sake" (5:10).—Jesus declared that the kingdom of heaven belongs also to those who are persecuted for upholding God's standards of justice, truth, and goodness. Persecution often comes to those who, in the name of God, oppose the evil in the world. Jesus did not promise a present-day reward for the persecuted. But he assured them that the only king-

dom which will always remain belongs to them.

"You when men revile you and persecute you . . . on my account" *(5:11-12).*—This ninth and last Beatitude is really an expansion of the one preceding it and is often included with it. Here Jesus was telling his disciples what the consequences of following him might be. In the case of these followers, being persecuted for righteousness' sake would mean being persecuted for being a disciple of Jesus. When he was physically gone from earth, the world's hatred would focus on his disciples.

People would revile them, persecute them, and speak evil against them falsely because they were Jesus' followers. A person may be persecuted for doing what is wrong. A Christian should face persecution only because he or she is a follower of Jesus.

Surprisingly, Jesus told his disciples to rejoice at such persecution, remembering the prophets who had faced the same harsh treatment from the world in their day. The reward they would have in heaven would be great.

Salt and Light (5:13-16)

Jesus went on to teach that his disciples' functions in the world are like those of salt and light.

"You are the salt of the earth" *(5:13).*—In calling his disciples "the salt of the earth" Jesus was describing their work in the world. The ancient world considered salt very important, since salt kept food from spoiling. Like food, the society of earth needs an antidote for its decay, or corruption. The disciples of Jesus are to be this antidote.

Salt is different from the food into which it is put. The disciples, too, differ from the world in which they live. The disciples of Jesus give flavor and meaning to the world, even as salt seasons food.

Jesus warned that salt which has "lost its taste" is fit only to be trodden upon. When a Christian stops being different from the world and no longer works against the forces of decay, he has stopped being salt to the earth. He will have no positive influence on the world.

"You are the light of the world . . ." *(5:14-16).*—Jesus himself is the "true light" (John 1:9) and "the light of the world" (John 8:12). But he also called his disciples "the light of the world" (v. 14). They could not help radiating the light that came from him, just as a city situated on a hilltop cannot be hidden.

If light is covered up, it might as well not exist. Who would put a lighted lamp under a meal-tub ("bushel," v. 15) instead of on a stand? Hidden, a lamp gives no light to the house's occupants.

Christians sometimes try to hide their light from the world's darkness. But Jesus was saying they are to shine in the darkness, dispelling the darkness with loving service. They are to make their influence as Christians felt in the world. Their motive is not, however, to draw attention to themselves. Instead they are to lead people to give glory to God, who is the source of their works (v. 16).

The Place of the Jewish Law (5:17-20)

Jesus told his hearers that he had definitely not come to do away with "the law and the prophets" (v. 17), God's earlier revelation of himself and his will. Instead, he had come "to fulfil them" (v. 17). How was he going to fulfill them? He alone would carry out God's purpose and intention in giving the law and the prophets. He would lead people to a righteousness higher than that achieved by keeping the letter of the law.

Jesus declared that "not an iota" (the smallest of the Greek letters) or "a dot" (a tiny stroke in a Hebrew letter) would "pass from the law" before the whole law had been fulfilled (v. 18). Doing what God has commanded, then, is of the greatest importance.

But Jesus included a warning. His disciples' righteousness would have to be greater than that of the scribes and Pharisees. Otherwise, his disciples would not enter God's kingdom, for they would not really be living under God's rule.

The Pharisees and scribes devoted their lives to the study and keeping of the law. Who could be more righteous than they? Jesus knew that when a person lives by the strict letter of the law, the requirements upon him are limited. He can do a definite thing to satisfy a definite legal requirement. But Jesus wanted his disciples to live by a higher righteousness, one which knows no legal limits.

Jesus went on to describe the kind of higher righteousness he required of his followers. Verses 21-48 contain some of Jesus' basic teachings about higher righteousness.

A New Look at the Law Against Murder (5:21-26)

Jesus reminded those to whom he was speaking that one of the Ten Commandments forbade murder. But he went on to deepen the requirements of that commandment. He saw that attitudes of hatred, anger, and contempt lay behind the act of murder. And he considered these attitudes so seriously wrong that he suggested they should be as punishable as the actual act of murder. Of course no court on earth would be capable of trying a person for his attitude alone.

Jesus declared that a person should face judgment for being angry at a brother. If a person's anger had progressed to the point of insulting a brother, that person deserved to be tried by the council, or Sanhedrin. A person whose rage caused him to call his brother a fool was deserving of "the hell of fire" (v. 22). Jesus meant that when one person has contempt for another, he is seeing that person as less than completely human. Murder grows out of such an attitude.

Jesus stressed the importance of quickly settling differences with one's brother. He gave two illustrations.

Religious Jews went to Jerusalem to present their offering at the Temple. Jesus said that if, at the altar, the worshiper remembered that he had somehow offended his brother, he should leave his offering at the altar. He should then go and come to a reconciliation with his brother before making his gift to God (vv. 23-24). It is impossible for a person to truly worship God while being at odds with his brother.

In the second illustration, really a small parable, Jesus pictured a man on the way to court with his accuser, perhaps a person to whom he owed a debt. Jesus emphasized the need for settling with the accuser before the case came before the court and punishment was handed down (vv. 25-26).

Jesus meant for his hearers to understand that we are all on our way to God's court. Christians should settle any differences with others in this life. Reconciliation with others shows a right relationship with God.

The Problems of Adultery and Divorce (5:27-32)

The problem of adultery (5:27-30).—Jesus next reinterpreted the commandment forbidding adultery. He began by declaring that his hearers knew the law "You shall not commit adultery" (v. 27; see Ex. 20:14).

According to the Jewish law, a married woman was guilty of adultery if she were unfaithful to her husband. A man, however, whether married or not, was considered guilty of adultery only if his partner was the wife of another man. In that case, he was thought to have violated that man's property rights.

But Jesus taught that it was not enough to refrain from the act of adultery. Lust, too, is wrong and, in fact, is the beginning point for actually committing adultery (v. 28). Lust and love are opposites. Lust causes one person to treat another as an object rather than as a person, sacred in God's sight. Here Jesus was also including another of the Ten Commandments, that which forbade coveting the wife of another man (see Deut. 5:21).

Jesus saw lust as such a serious and damaging problem that he felt radical discipline was necessary to free oneself from it. A person should get rid of whatever is causing him to sin, however great the sacrifice might be. Jesus spoke metaphorically, saying it would be better to go through life without an eye or hand than to have "your whole body go into hell" (v. 30).

The problem of divorce (5:31-32).—Jesus then explored a related problem, that of divorce. According to Jewish law, a man could divorce his wife, but a wife could not divorce her husband. To give some protection to wives, the law required a husband to give the wife he was divorcing "a certificate of divorce" (v. 31).

In Jesus' day one school of thought held that a man could divorce his wife for any reason, however trivial. The other held that only adultery was sufficient reason for divorce. Jesus opposed divorce completely, except when the wife had committed adultery. (Mark and Luke do not mention this exception.) In that case, the marriage would already have been broken.

Jesus' words in verse 32 have been the subject of much controversy. There he seems to have taught that anyone who divorced his wife for any reason except adultery made her an adulteress and made any man who later married her an adulterer. It seems unlikely that Jesus was saying that God would judge an innocent woman and man guilty of this sin. More likely he was saying that in divorcing his innocent wife, the husband had treated her as he would have treated an adulteress, thus stigmatizing her later marriage to another man.

Jesus was raising the position of women and of marriage to a new high. He was saying that marriage should be a permanent commitment, not a temporary contract.

Jesus' word about marriage and divorce are meant to reveal God's ideal will for those who are trying to live as citizens of God's kingdom. These words stress the seriousness with which marriage should be undertaken and maintained. But even here, failure to attain that ideal does not rule out God's forgiveness.

Oath Taking (5:33-37)

Jesus reminded his hearers that the Old Testament permitted oath taking and required that any promise sworn to should be kept (v. 33). In Jesus' day, however, the scribes had made some oaths less binding than others.

Any oath which made use of God's name was considered absolutely binding. For fear of not being able to keep the promise made, a person might swear by Jerusalem, by heaven, by earth, or something else. If God's name was not used, the promise need not be kept.

Jesus totally rejected this practice. He declared that everything has a connection with God, anyway. Heaven, for example, is God's throne; earth is God's footstool (v. 35). God is present whenever any transaction takes place, whether his name is used or not.

So Jesus told his followers not to take oaths. A person of integrity, one whose word can be trusted, has no need for them. A simple Yes or No should be enough without any oath (v. 37).

Notice that Jesus was not talking about profanity in this instance. And he did not mean that his followers were to refuse to take oaths in court. He was simply appealing for truthfulness in all that a person might say.

How to Overcome Evil (5:38-42)

Jesus quoted part of the Old Testament law of retaliation, " 'An eye for an eye and a tooth for a tooth' " (v. 38; see Lev. 24:17-20). Harsh as this law sounds, it actually prevented an excess of punishment for a given offense. It stipulated that the punishment was to be in proportion to the crime committed.

But Jesus declared that his followers were to live by a higher law than this. He told them, "Do not resist one who is evil" (v. 39). This statement is a hard one to understand, since Jesus spent his entire ministry resisting evil. Probably Jesus' words should be understood as meaning, "Don't resist evil with evil." Evil cannot be overcome with more evil. Jesus gave three examples to illustrate his teaching.

He first told his listeners that if someone struck them on their right cheek, they should turn the other cheek also (v. 39). To strike someone on the right cheek, a person must usually hit with the back of his right hand. This act was considered an especially insulting one by the Jews.

Jesus was talking about more than a literal physical blow here, however. What he said could apply to any kind of insult or humiliation a Christian might face. How should a Christian meet such treatment? To return evil for evil would not help the situation at all. Jesus advised against responding in a spirit of hatred and revenge. To turn the other cheek could mean to act in a positive way for the good of the one who has given the insult.

In his second illustration, Jesus gave an example taken from Jewish law. He declared that if someone sued one of his followers for his coat, that follower should freely give up his cloak also (v. 40). Jewish law allowed a person to sue a debtor for his coat, which was an inner garment. The law forbade suing for a person's cloak, however. The cloak was an outer garment, worn during the day and used at night by the poor as a bed covering. Jesus meant that in dealing with others, his followers were to be willing to give even more than the law could take from them.

Jesus then taught that a Christian forced by someone to walk one mile should go ahead and travel two miles with that person (v. 41). In Jesus' day, a Roman soldier could force a Jew to carry his pack for one mile. Just think of the hateful feelings a Jew would have had toward the soldier who forced him to do this! Think how happy he would have been when his mile of forced labor ended! But Jesus said a follower of his shouldn't stop at one forced mile. Instead, he should freely and voluntarily go another mile.

Jesus was teaching his disciples to let generosity, not the desire for revenge, rule their relationships with others. A Christian should willingly do more than he can be forced to do.

In keeping with this teaching on generosity in actions, Jesus also taught that his followers are to be generous toward those who might come to them in need (v. 42). They are to think about how they can help meet another's need rather than about whether that other person deserves help.

Paul later summed up Jesus' teaching in this passage when he wrote, "Do not be overcome by evil, but overcome evil with good" (Rom. 12:21). Jesus was not calling for a passive acceptance of evil. He was calling for meeting evil with positive good and so overcoming the evil.

How to Treat an Enemy (5:43-48)

Jesus' next and closely related teaching was about the higher righteousness he required of his followers concerning treatment of an enemy. The Old Testament law commanded love for one's neighbor (see Lev. 19:18). The Jews usually interpreted "neighbor" as meaning only a fellow Jew. The law did not specifically call for hatred of one's enemy. When Jesus declared "You have heard that it was said" (v. 43) that one's neighbor should be loved and one's enemy hated, he was doubtless referring to the attitude which condoned hatred not only of enemies but of people such as Samaritans as well.

Jesus refuted this attitude. He called for love for one's enemies and prayer for one's persecutors (v. 44). To act in such a loving way, even toward enemies, would mark a person as a child of God, having in his or her nature some of the characteristics of God himself (v. 45). After all, God (Jesus said) sends his good gifts of sunshine and rain on the good and the bad, on the unjust and the just (v. 45). He shows an impartial attitude of goodwill toward all people, whether they love him or not. Christians are also to do good to all people, even to their enemies.

There is nothing unusual about loving someone who loves us. Even those who don't know God love those who love them (vv. 46-47). But it takes a special act of the will to love those who hate us or who have persecuted us. Only in showing such love can a Christian prove he knows God's love.

Jesus told his disciples, "You, therefore, must be perfect, as your heavenly Father is perfect" (v. 48). The word *perfect* here has caused a great deal of misunderstanding. Going by the context, it seems Jesus meant that his followers are, like God, to show love to all people, being all-inclusive in their goodwill. In his version of this same passage, Luke used a word which has been translated "merciful" (Luke 6:36) in place of "perfect." The same thought seems to be present here.

How to Give Gifts (6:1-4)

Jesus went on to warn against practicing one's religion in order to be seen by other people. He declared that when one's motive in religious practice is to have others see one's superiority, that person can expect no reward from God. Verse 1 really introduces the first eighteen verses of chapter 6. It could equally well preface verses 5 and 16.

Verses 2-4 deal with the practice of giving charitable gifts. The Jewish law did not require almsgiving, and so this practice was considered especially praiseworthy. Jesus said that the "hypocrites" sounded a trumpet before them when they gave alms, whether to beggars on the street or in the synagogue collection (v. 2). Sounding the trumpet was likely a figurative way of saying that they found ways of calling others' attention to what they were doing.

These people didn't want to give alms unless they could be seen and praised for their generosity. Their motive wasn't to help others or to show gratitude to God. In calling them "hypocrites," Jesus was saying that they were like actors in a play, acting out a part. He declared that the praise they received from people was all the reward they would get (v. 2).

Jesus instructed his disciples to give alms in such a way that their left hands would not know what their right hands were doing. This secret giving would be seen and rewarded by their heavenly Father.

In Matthew 5:16, Jesus had told his followers to let others see their good works. Is there a conflict here? Jesus wanted the world to see the good works of his disciples. But he did not want his disciples to do good works just so that they themselves would be seen by the world.

All charitable gifts do not have to be given in secret. But if a person is tempted to give just so that others can see him and praise his religious superiority, he should make a practice of a secret giving seen by God alone.

The Matter of Prayer (6:5-15)

Jesus saw prayer as a second religious practice which, like almsgiving, could be carried out with the wrong motive and in the wrong way. Devout Jews prayed at three set hours of the day, and prayer was an important part of their lives.

Jesus warned that his disciples should not be guilty of praying the way the "hypocrites" prayed. These men managed to be in a visible, public place at the times of prayer. Their motive in praying was to be seen by others. Jesus declared that that public attention was the only reward these people would receive.

For Jesus, prayer was a personal and private communication with God. He told his disciples to pray in private, and God would see and reward their secret prayers (v. 6). Jesus was not condemning all public prayer but was saying that prayer should be a personal effort to know and conform to God's will, not a method of getting people's attention and praise.

Jesus criticized those who, in praying, repetitiously heaped up meaningless, empty phrases. These people, like pagans, thought God would be more likely to answer a long, babbling prayer.

This kind of prayer showed a lack of trust in the Father. After all, Jesus said, God knows our needs even before we ask him. He already wants what is best for us. Prayer is not for the purpose of informing God of our needs or compelling him to do what we want. Instead, it is for the purpose of putting ourselves in line with God's will.

Jesus went on to give an example of the kind of prayer his disciples should pray. This prayer has become known as the Lord's Prayer or the Model Prayer.

"Our Father who art in heaven" (6:9).—Jesus knew God as his own Father, and he taught his disciples to trust in him as their Father as well. God is not a remote being who doesn't care. He is our Father who loves us, knows our needs, and wants to help us. At the same time, God is a transcendent being who is "in heaven" and who deserves our reverence. Jesus addressed his prayer to One who is near and responsive as our Father and yet majestic in his power.

"Hallowed be thy name" (6:9).—In Hebrew thought, the name stood for the person. So this first petition of the prayer is a plea that all people may come to regard God as holy and live lives devoted to him. It may actually be a prayer that God will quickly bring history to an end so that all people will know his holiness.

"Thy kingdom come./Thy will be done,/On earth as it is in heaven" (6:10).—These two petitions are closely related and have almost the same meaning. The second may be intended as an explanation of the first.

God's kingdom, or his rule, will come in its fullness when the forces of evil have all been defeated. This request is that this victory over evil will become a reality.

God's rule cannot come until God's will is done, both in our lives and in the world. In the perfection of heaven, God's will is now done. This prayer asks that God's will be done and his rule be acknowledged on earth even as it already is in heaven.

"Give us this day our daily bread" (6:11).—From this point on, the prayer's petitions have to do with people's needs. Jesus recognized that his followers needed food and other essentials. In this petition, "our" means that the prayer is for all others as well as for ourselves. "Daily" means that which is necessary for the immediate future, perhaps for the coming day. "Bread" means those things necessary for physical life. This part of the prayer acknowledges our ultimate dependence on God's generosity for all our needs.

"And forgive us our debts,/As we also have forgiven our debtors" (6:12).—This petition sees us as debtors before God because of our sins. This part of the prayer is a plea that God will forgive the sins we have committed. At the same time it acknowledges that we cannot expect to receive God's forgiveness unless we show forgiveness toward those who have wronged us. If we realize our own indebtedness to God, we can hardly fail to forgive others their lesser debts to us.

"And lead us not into temptation,/But deliver us from evil" (6:13).—The previous petition of the Lord's Prayer asked forgiveness for sins one had committed. This petition asks for strength not to commit future sins.

God does not tempt people (see Jas. 1:13). However, he does allow his people to be led into situations which will test their faithfulness. The word translated "temptation" can also mean "trial." This part of the prayer is a plea that God will not lead us to face tests or trials which will cause us to be unfaithful to him.

The word translated "evil" can mean either evil in a general sense or "the evil one," Satan. This second part of the petition actually repeats the thought of the first part.

Notice that the familiar closing of the Lord's Prayer, "For thine is the kingdom . . ." is not found in modern translations. The best and earliest manuscripts of Matthew's Gospel do not contain these words. It seems probable that very early Christians added this beautiful closing when they used this prayer in their worship.

An additional note (6:14-15).—These two verses contain an explanation of the prayer for forgiveness of sins (v. 12). When a person has an unforgiving spirit toward others, he is incapable of receiving God's forgiveness for himself. Jesus said, then, that a person who does not forgive will not be forgiven.

Fasting (6:16-18)

Fasting (abstaining from food for a period of time) is the third of the religious practices Jesus warned about in chapter 6. Like almsgiving and prayer, fasting must come from the right motive or it loses its value.

Jesus declared that the hypocrites made a conspicuous production out of their fasting. They disfigured their faces and looked dismal to call attention to their fast. They wanted everyone to know they were fasting. This attention, Jesus said, was the only reward they would receive.

Jesus wanted his disciples to behave differently. He told them to behave normally when they fasted. They were to anoint their heads (symbolizing joy) and wash their faces. God alone would know about their secret act of devotion, and their reward would come from him.

True and Lasting Riches (6:19-21)

Jesus wanted people to have life's material necessities. But he knew the dangers of making the accumulation of material things the goal of one's life. Riches could become a person's god— a very unreliable god at that.

Jesus taught that there is no final security in earthly possessions. Moth, rust, and thieves can quickly do away with whatever wealth people have managed to accumulate (v. 19). People need to devote their attention to acquiring "treasures in heaven" (v. 20) rather than on earth. Only heavenly treasures endure both now and when earthly life is over. What are heavenly treasures? Service to God and kind and merciful deeds done to others are examples of this lasting wealth.

Jesus declared that a person's heart would be where his or her treasure is (v. 21). The "heart" includes the mind and the will. People tend to devote their minds and wills to those things which are most important to them. And they share the destiny of the things to which they have devoted themselves—whether to things which last or to things which perish.

The Lamp of the Body (6:22-23)

The physical eye brings either light or darkness into the body, depending on the eye's state of health. The inner being, too, has an eye, a spiritual eye.

If the spiritual eye is focused on God, it is a sound eye, bringing God's light into the person's being. But if that spiritual eye is trying to focus on both God and worldly values at the same time, the eye becomes unsound. Spiritual vision will be blurred. In that case, spiritual darkness instead of light will fill the person.

The Choice of a Master (6:24)

Jesus went on to teach that no one person can be a slave to two masters at the same time. People have the choice of serving God or serving mammon (an Aramaic word meaning money or material things). The pursuit of wealth is such an all-absorbing one that it will enslave a person. Then there will be no room for God in that person's life. God and mammon each demand full allegiance.

Jesus did not teach that money is evil. Money has many uses, some good and some bad. Jesus did condemn the life-style which devotes itself to accumulating wealth instead of to serving God. It is the love of money, not money itself, which is the root of evil (see 1 Tim. 6:10).

First Things First (6:25-34)

People who have made service to God their life goal do not need to worry about material things, Jesus taught. Remember that he was speaking primarily to those who had given up material security to follow him. How would their needs be met?

Jesus warned his followers against anxiety concerning food and clothing. He declared that life consists of more than food and clothes. He reminded his disciples about God's provision for the birds of the air, far less valuable to God than human beings (vv. 25-26).

Jesus was not suggesting that his followers be idle or fail to make provision for the future. He was condemning anxiety and the lack of faith anxiety expressed. A person who has made money his god has to be anxious. At any moment his god may prove inadequate. But the person who, in faith, has put God first has no need for anxiety.

Jesus reminded his hearers that anxiety cannot even add a slight amount to the length of a person's life (v. 27). In fact anxiety may actually shorten life.

To illustrate the futility of anxiety about clothing, Jesus reminded his followers about the lilies of the field. Their life span is very short, but God clothes them beautifully. Won't he also take care of the needs of those who have given their lives to him? (vv. 28-30).

Anxiety over food, clothing, and the future is pagan, Jesus taught. God knows all the needs of his children (vv. 31-32). Put God and his rule first in your life, and he will see that your other needs are met (v. 33).

It is necessary to take some forethought for the future. But anxiety about tomorrow is useless. Every day, Jesus said, has troubles enough of its own. So don't let yourself be burdened by anxiety concerning a future over which you have no control (v. 34).

Judgment and Discernment (7:1-6)

Jesus warned that his disciples were not to judge. Some kinds of judgment are necessary, but Jesus was warning against unloving, condemning criticism of another person. He declared that God will judge a person with the same measure of severity that person has used to judge others (vv. 1-2).

To judge another person is to take on a role for which only God is qualified. Only God can see beyond the outward appearance to underlying causes and motives.

Jesus wanted to show how wrong it is to judge others. So he painted a comical verbal picture : A person with a log sticking out of his own eye is trying to remove the tiny speck he sees in his brother's eye (vv. 3-4).

Jesus meant that it is ridiculous and hypocritical for a person with a large fault of his own to criticize another for some small failing. How can he help his brother rid himself of his failing if he has not first realized his own failings and need for God's mercy? No doubt

Jesus was thinking of some of the Pharisees who made themselves judges of the righteousness of others, not realizing their own spiritual faults.

Harsh judgment of another is wrong. But in his very next statement, Jesus taught that his disciples should show discernment. As followers of Jesus, his disciples should share his message with all who would receive it. But they should be careful not to indiscriminately spread the holy message to those who would only ridicule it and become more hostile toward it.

Jesus declared, in effect, that some people cannot appreciate what is holy. He used the examples of dogs and swine to illustrate the point. Dogs cannot tell the difference between "what is holy" (possibly meat which had been offered for sacrifice) and what is not (v. 6). And if a person threw pearls before swine, the swine would become enraged at being tricked into thinking the pearls were food (such as peas or acorns). Having no idea of the worth of the pearls, they would trample them and attack the one who had thrown the pearls to them (v. 6). A follower of Jesus, then, should use loving discernment in deciding when, how, and with whom to share the truths of Jesus.

Asking, Seeking, Knocking (7:7-12)

Jesus taught that his disciples should "ask," "seek," and "knock" (v. 7). These present imperative forms imply that a person is to keep on asking, seeking, and knocking. Jesus was stressing the need for persistence in prayer. That persistence would be an indication of seriousness in making the request and of faith that God would answer.

Jesus told his followers that those who ask will receive. Those who seek will find. A door will be opened to those who knock (vv. 7-8). Notice that Jesus did not say a person would necessarily receive what he asked for. But he did teach that persistent prayer would bring an answer.

A person need not fear that God will give something bad in response to prayer. If a son asks his father for bread, no father worthy of the name will give him a stone instead, Jesus declared. Neither will the father give his son a serpent if he asks for a fish (vv. 9-10). In the same way, God gives only good gifts to those who come to him in prayer (v. 11).

Likewise, God's children are to do good things for others. Jesus put the sum of the law and the prophets into the statement we call the Golden Rule: "Whatever you wish that men would do to you, do so to them" (v. 12). This saying was already known to the Jews in negative form. Jesus changed it into positive, active form. His followers were not simply to keep from doing to another that which they did not want done to themselves. They were to treat others in the same way they would like for those others to treat them.

This rule is meant for those who live under the rule of God, not for the world at large. Only a person whose will is submitted to God can care as much about another's welfare as about his own.

The Wide and Narrow Gates (7:13-14)

Jesus taught that there are two differing paths a person may follow. Most people, with little thought, enter the wide gate and follow the easy, wide way. It takes a definite, conscious act of the will to choose to enter the narrow gate and to follow the difficult narrow way.

The narrow way is the path Jesus had been describing in the Sermon on the Mount. It is a way which demands submission to God, self-discipline, and the positive showing of love to others. The wide way makes no such demands. Yet, Jesus said, it leads to "destruction" (v. 13). In contrast, the hard, narrow way leads in the end to life for the few who find it (v. 14).

The True and the False (7:15-23)

Jesus knew his church would not be immune from the influence of false prophets. So he forewarned his followers about these. He wanted them to know that not all people who would claim to belong to Christ would actually be Christians. His followers needed to be able to distinguish between the true and the false.

Jesus foresaw false prophets who would appear, outwardly, to be genuine. They would appear to be part of the flock. Underneath their "sheep's clothing," however, they would be "ravenous wolves" (v. 15). Their aim would be to oppose Christ, not to further his kingdom. They would be greedy, ready to exploit others for their own selfish gain.

How could a Christian distinguish between a true prophet and a false one? Jesus gave only one criterion: their fruit (v. 16). Good trees bear fruit which is good. Bad trees are destroyed because they bear fruit which is not good (vv. 17-20).

Jesus' whole sermon to this point had been a description of the good fruit which should characterize his followers' lives. A true prophet, a true Christian, would have these characteristics. A false one would not.

Jesus went on to say that some people who think they are citizens of the kingdom are really not. They may have done religious works, even worked miracles in Christ's name. But real faith is expressed in obedience to God. If they have not done God's will, Christ will declare in the day of judgment that he never knew them (vv. 21-23).

The Parable of the Two Builders (7:24-27)

Jesus was reaching the end of his sermon. He knew that some who heard him would become true disciples. They would make him and his teachings the foundation of their lives. Others, probably most, would hear but not obey.

Jesus told a parable to illustrate the difference between those who would only hear and those who would hear and do as he had told them.

Two men set out to build themselves houses, Jesus told his hearers. One man, a wise man, "built his house upon the rock" (v. 24). It was harder to build there. But when the wind and floods came, he was glad he had taken the hard way. His house stood. Jesus likened this man to those who both heard and obeyed his words (vv. 24-25).

The second man took the easy way out in building his house. He built his house on the sand, and it looked secure enough. But when the wind and floods came, his house fell.

Jesus declared that that is the case with a person whose life is not built on him and his teachings (vv. 26-27). The winds and floods may refer to the storms of the last judgment. More likely they symbolize all the storms, crises, and testings of life. When difficult times come, the life built on Christ and his Word will be able to weather the storm.

The Crowd's Estimation of Jesus (7:28-29)

At the end of Jesus' Sermon on the Mount, the listening crowd expressed astonishment. They had heard their scribes quote past authorities. But Jesus spoke with a power and authority which commanded their attention and their respect.

Mighty Works and Words of Power
8:1 to 9:34

Jesus' Healing of a Leper (8:1-4)

In his sermon there on the mountain, Jesus had been speaking of his relationship to the Jewish law. He had declared both his loyalty to that law and his expectation that his followers would go far beyond the mere keeping of the letter of the law. As Jesus descended from the mountain, followed by the crowds, he was given an opportunity to show concretely how he viewed the law.

Matthew wrote that "a leper came to him and knelt before him" (v. 2). The leper's coming to Jesus was in itself a violation of the law of Moses, since lepers were considered unclean. What was leprosy? It seems that in Bible times the term *leprosy* covered a variety of skin ailments, possibly including the disease now known as leprosy. Leprosy was considered the worst of diseases in ancient times.

Leviticus 13 contains the rules for diagnosing and dealing with leprosy. A leper was required to wear torn clothing, let his hair hang loose, stay away from people who did not have leprosy, and cry "Unclean, unclean" (Lev. 13:45-46). The social isolation associated with leprosy made it an especially dreaded disease. Leviticus 14 contains the rules for the offerings to be made when (as was unlikely) a person no longer had the disease.

The leper who met Jesus knew the anguish both of disease and of separation from others. He believed that Jesus could cure his sickness. He declared, "if you will, you can make me clean" (v. 2). Jesus then reached out and, assuring the leper of his willingness, touched and healed him immediately (v. 3). The law forbade touching a leper. To Jesus, however, the suffering man's need for healing had priority over the keeping of the details of the religious regulations.

Jesus told the now-healed leper to tell no one about the miracle. He did not want to be followed just because of his miracles. And it

was important that the authorities not become too hostile toward
him at this early stage of his ministry.

But to demonstrate his respect for the law, Jesus told the man to
follow the rules laid down by Moses for healed lepers. The man was
to go to the priest and present the prescribed offering. Then he could
once again live as a member of his family and community.

The Healing of a Gentile's Servant (8:5-13)

As Jesus reached Capernaum, the headquarters for his Galilean
ministry, a centurion came out to meet him. The centurion told Jesus
that his slave was paralyzed and "in terrible distress" (v. 6). This centurion was a Gentile officer in the Roman army, likely in Herod
Antipas' service. It went against Jewish regulations for a Jew to enter
a Gentile home. Yet Jesus immediately offered to go to the centurion's home and heal the slave.

Knowing about the Jewish law, the centurion declared that he
was unworthy to have Jesus under his roof. But he recognized in
Jesus an authority which could come only from God. He told Jesus
that as a Roman soldier, he understood authority. He was a man
both under authority himself and with authority to command
others. He believed that Jesus had the authority to heal his slave with
just a word, without even going near the sick man.

Jesus was amazed at this Gentile's faith. It exceeded the faith he
had found among God's own people, the Jews. He foretold that
many "from east and west" (v. 11), Gentiles, would share in the joy
of God's kingdom. Yet many Jews who, as Abraham's descendants
expected to be included, would instead find themselves in "the outer
darkness," (v. 12).

In response to the centurion's faith, Jesus told the man he had
answered his request. Right then the centurion's slave was healed.

Other Healings (8:14-17)

Simon Peter had a house in Capernaum. When Jesus went into
Peter's house, he saw that Peter's mother-in-law was bedridden,
"sick with a fever" (v. 14). She may have had malaria.

Jesus healed the woman by touching her hand. The fever left, and
her strength returned immediately. Right away, she began serving
Jesus, who was a guest in the house.

This small miracle contains at least three important ideas for us. First, it shows Jesus healing a woman. Women did not hold a position of much importance in the society of that day. But Jesus valued them equally with men. Second, this was a privately done miracle. Jesus performed his miracles out of compassion, not out of a desire for publicity. Finally, a person who has been touched and healed by Jesus, whether physically or spiritually, will want to serve him.

That same night, Jesus healed many other people who were brought to him. Matthew wrote that these healings fulfilled Isaiah's prophecy (Isa. 53:4) about the One who was to be God's Suffering Servant: " 'He took our infirmities and bore our diseases' " (v. 17). Jesus saw disease as something opposed to God's will. Each time he healed a person, he was doing battle with the forces of evil.

Two Who Wanted to Follow (8:18-22)

Thronged by crowds whose main interest was in his miracles, Jesus decided to cross to the other side of the Sea of Galilee. Before he could do so, two would-be followers spoke to him.

The first of these men was a scribe. He assured Jesus that he would follow him anywhere he might go. Jesus recognized in the man's confident enthusiasm a failure to realize just what following him might involve. Jesus pointed out the fact that even birds and foxes have places of refuge. But Jesus, the Son of man, had no earthly place of security.

Verse 20 marks Jesus' first use, in Matthew's Gospel, of the term "Son of man" to describe himself. Usually this term simply meant man. However, after the use of the phrase in the book of Daniel, it had become a messianic title. Daniel 7:13-14 described "one like a son of man" coming "with the clouds of heaven" and being given by God an indestructible kingdom. "Son of man" was a title which expressed both Jesus' humanity and his future triumph but which lacked the political implications attached to the title "messiah."

The second disciple wanted to follow Jesus, but only after he had taken care of other obligations. He told Jesus that first he had to bury his father (v. 21). Very probably he meant that he needed to care for his father until his father's death. The Jewish law considered it a son's duty to care for his father in his old age and then give him burial.

Jesus believed that his mission and that of his disciples was so urgent that it superseded even this sacred obligation. Those who were dead spiritually (those who had not received Jesus' life-giving message) could bury the physically dead (v. 22). Those who had received the good news and become spiritually alive should consider following Jesus to be their primary obligation.

Jesus' Calming of a Storm (8:23-27)

Jesus and his disciples got on board a boat for the trip across the Sea of Galilee. But the journey proved to be a hazardous one. A sudden storm arose, and waves began to engulf the boat. Jesus, meanwhile, slept in spite of the storm.

His frightened disciples awakened him, begging him to save them from the storm's danger. Jesus chided them for their fear and lack of belief. Then he stood and calmed the waves and the wind. Naturally his disciples were amazed. Here was a man who was obeyed even by the forces of nature.

The psalmist had declared that God's ability to calm the sea was one of his greatest powers (Ps. 89:9). Now Matthew was ascribing that same power to Jesus. This story tells us that Jesus is with us in all of life's storms. We are to have faith and not be afraid, since no storm is beyond his control.

Jesus' Healing of Two Demon-Possessed Men (8:28-34)

On the eastern side of the Sea of Galilee was "the country of the Gadarenes" (v. 28). When Jesus arrived there, he was met by two demon-possessed men. These mentally deranged men lived among the tombs which were probably cut into the side of a mountain. So violent were these men that everyone was afraid to go near the area they inhabited.

The demons possessing these men recognized Jesus and his power to destroy them. They asked why he had come to bring them torment before the end time, the day of judgment.

A large herd of swine was in the area, indicating that this was a Gentile region. The demons, realizing that Jesus could destroy them, asked Jesus to send them into the swine. They did not want to remain disembodied when cast out of the men they possessed.

Jesus did as they requested, but the result was not what the demons had hoped. The swine rushed headlong down the bank and drowned in the water. By this miracle, which left the two men cured, Jesus demonstrated his authority over the forces of evil.

Those who had been tending the swine carried the news of what Jesus had done into the city (probably Gadara). The city's inhabitants came out to see Jesus. But they did not rejoice that the two men had been made well. Instead, perhaps fearing Jesus' power, they begged him to leave the area. It seems that the loss of property mattered more to them than the restoration of two of their fellowmen.

A Paralytic's Forgiveness and Healing (9:1-8)

After Jesus arrived back in Capernaum, "they brought to him a paralytic, lying on his bed" (v. 2). It was obvious that the man needed physical healing. But Jesus saw that the man needed forgiveness of his sins even more.

The man's sin was not necessarily the direct cause of his handicap, though sin ultimately is at the root of all sickness and death. However, Jesus may have seen that forgiveness was necessary before the man could be healed. In response to "their faith" (v. 2), (probably the faith of those who had brought the man), Jesus pronounced the man's sins forgiven.

Some scribes who were present thought that Jesus' pronouncement was blasphemy. They reasoned that since only God could forgive sins, Jesus was taking upon himself one of the prerogatives of God.

Jesus knew their thoughts. So he asked them whether it was easier to tell a paralyzed man his sins had been forgiven or to tell him to walk. It would be hard to prove that forgiveness had actually taken place. Healing, on the other hand, could be easily demonstrated.

Referring to himself as the Son of man, Jesus declared that he would heal the man as proof of his authority to forgive. He then told the paralytic to rise, take up his bed, and go to his home. The paralytic did as Jesus had told him.

Such power amazed the watching crowd. This miracle caused them to give glory to God because he had delegated his power "to men" (v. 8). In Jesus, they had seen God at work. Jesus' works of healing and forgiving were signs that God's kingdom was dawning, that God's order was being restored.

The Call of Matthew (9:9-13)

Passing by "the tax office" (v. 9) or customs house in Capernaum,

Jesus saw Matthew, a Jewish tax collector. Matthew, who was probably in the service of Herod Antipas, may have levied taxes on passing caravans or on such local industries as fishing. Tax collectors were an especially despised group of people. You see, the highest bidder got the job of tax collector in an area. He then had to charge enough in taxes to make a profit over what he had spent to get the job. Corruption in tax collection was widespread.

Yet Jesus accepted Matthew and called him to follow as his disciple. It is likely that Jesus and Matthew had had some contact before this time. But this meeting marked Jesus' call for Matthew to make a final choice to become his follower. Matthew did choose to follow Jesus.

As Jesus and his disciples sat eating, "many tax collectors and sinners" joined them (v. 10). According to Luke's account of this incident, the occasion was a dinner to which Matthew had invited Jesus (see Luke 5:29, where Matthew is called Levi). The Pharisees could not understand why Jesus would eat with these people since such contact was forbidden by their laws. They questioned Jesus' disciples about this.

Jesus himself heard and answered them. People who are well, he told them, do not need a doctor. Only sick people do. He suggested that the Pharisees go back and study Hosea 6:6, " 'I desire mercy, and not sacrifice' " (v. 13). The Pharisees were so intent on the perfect keeping of their rituals that they had neglected showing mercy to others. Jesus concluded by telling them, perhaps with irony in his voice, that he had come to call sinners, not the "righteous," like the Pharisees, who did not recognize their need (v. 13).

"Sinners," by the way, were not always immoral people. The Pharisees classed as "sinners" the ordinary people who failed to keep all the rituals the Pharisees said their laws required.

A Question About Fasting (9:14-17)

Some disciples of John the Baptist came to Jesus to ask a question. Both they and the Pharisees fasted, but Jesus and his disciples did not make a practice of fasting. John's disciples wanted to know why.

In the Old Testament, fasting was usually a spontaneous expression of mourning, repentance, or supplication in a time of crisis. By Jesus' time, however, the Pharisees fasted twice a week to show their religious merit. John's disciples evidently followed this practice as well.

Jesus had no objections to fasting and at times fasted himself. He believed, however, that a person should fast only when the occasion warranted it and not as a mechanical ritual.

Using the analogy of a wedding, Jesus declared that wedding guests do not mourn while the bridegroom is still present. He was the bridegroom, the Messiah. His disciples were the wedding guests, present at the dawning of the age of the Messiah. How could they fast when they still knew the joy of his presence?

Jesus declared that later, the bridegroom would be "taken away from them" (v. 15). He was referring here for the first time in Matthew's Gospel, to his death. When he was gone, it would be appropriate for his disciples to fast as a sign of mourning.

Fasting, as it was then practiced by the Pharisees, was only one example of the practices which could not be reconciled with the revolutionary new force Jesus' ministry was bringing into the world. Jesus gave two illustrations of the fact that Judaism as a whole could not contain his gospel.

A person would be foolish, he said, to sew "a piece of unshrunk cloth on an old garment" (v. 16). The first washing would surely cause the patch to tear away from the garment. A worse tear than the first would be made.

Likewise, no one would pour new wine into a brittle old wineskin. The ferment of the new wine would cause the old wineskin to burst. To preserve both the new wine and its container, a new wineskin must be used (v. 17)

The gospel Jesus brought could not be patched on to Judaism. Neither could it be contained within the old, legalistic forms. Only new forms could contain and express the new life Jesus was bringing.

Four Different Miracles (9:18-34)

A request to raise a daughter (9:18-19).—While Jesus was speaking to the disciples of John the Baptist, "a ruler" came to him and, kneeling before Jesus, asked him to raise his daughter who had "just died" (v. 18).

From Mark's parallel but more detailed account of this incident, we know that this man was a ruler of the synagogue and was named

Jairus (see Mark 5:22). This man strongly believed in Jesus' power even over death. Jesus and his disciples went at once with the man.

The healing of a woman with a long-term illness (9:20-22).—On the way, a woman in great need of healing "touched the fringe of his garment" (v. 20). This woman had had a hemorrhage for twelve long years. The Jewish law considered her "unclean" because of her illness, unfit to be out among people.

But this woman had faith in Jesus. She didn't want to call attention to her presence by asking him to heal her. Yet she believed that she would be healed if she could only touch his clothing. The "fringe" she touched was the tassle which Jews wore to remind them of God's commandments.

At the woman's touch, Jesus turned to look at her and declared that her faith had brought about her healing. That same moment, the woman did experience healing.

The raising of the ruler's daughter (9:23-26).—Reaching the home of the synagogue ruler, Jesus took note of the scene of mourning. The "flute players" and "crowd making a tumult" (v. 23) were the musicians and mourners it was customary to hire when a death had occurred.

Jesus ordered these to leave. He told them "the girl is not dead but sleeping" (v. 24). His words brought laughter from the hired mourners. Jesus' statement has been interpreted in varying ways by Bible scholars. Some take it literally, thinking Jesus meant the girl was not dead at all but simply in a coma which was mistaken for death. Others, probably more in line with Matthew's intention, think Jesus meant her death was not a final state. She could be awakened from death even as a person can be awakened from sleep.

When the mourners had been put out of the house, Jesus "went in and took her by the hand, and the girl arose" (v. 25). Naturally, news of this astounding miracle spread all over the district.

The restoring of two blind men's sight (9:27-31).—After Jesus left the ruler's house, two blind men met him and begged for healing. These men addressed him by the messianic title "Son of David" (v. 27). Jesus first made sure they believed he could heal them. Then, in response to their faith, he gave them their sight. The restoring of sight to the blind was a sign that the messianic age had begun (see Isa. 29:18).

Jesus sternly charged the men to tell no one of their healing. He did not want to be followed just for his miracles. But the men spread the good news anyway.

The healing of a mute (9:32-34).—A man who was "a dumb demoniac" (v. 32) was then brought to Jesus. This man was a mute, cut off from society by his inability to speak. His condition was then thought to be caused by a demon. Jesus cast out the demon, and to the amazement of the onlookers, the formerly mute man was able to speak.

The crowds declared that Israel had never before seen such works. But the attitude of the Pharisees was a different one. They couldn't deny that Jesus had worked miracles. So they declared that the devil, "the prince of demons" (v. 34) was the source of his power to cast out the demons.

The Mission of the Twelve
9:35 to 11:1

Jesus' Reason for Ministry (9:35-38)

Jesus taught, preached, and healed in villages and cities. The spiritual need of the crowds to whom he ministered called forth his compassion. He saw them as being "harassed and helpless, like sheep without a shepherd" (v. 36).

Sheep without a shepherd were totally helpless, with no protection from their enemies and no way to locate food. In the Old Testament, God's people were sometimes called his sheep. Jesus saw God's people harassed by their supposed religious leaders, as sheep are harassed by dogs and wolves. He saw that they lacked a shepherd who could protect the flock and bring it together for God. He himself intended to be that shepherd, as the fulfillment of Ezekiel 34:23.

Jesus told his disciples that he also saw the crowds in terms of a ripe harvest. The field of harvest was too great in proportion to the number of laborers who were available. If laborers were not found to do the harvesting, the "grain" would be lost. Yet he didn't tell his disciples to go out and recruit people to do the harvesting. Instead, he told them to pray that God, to whom the harvest belonged, would send laborers to gather the harvest.

A Listing of the Twelve (10:1-4)

Calling to him the twelve men who were his disciples, Jesus extended to them his authority over demons and diseases of all kinds. Matthew named the twelve who received this authority from Jesus. In verse 2 he called them "apostles," meaning those who were sent out. Their number, twelve, was reminiscent of the twelve tribes of Israel. These men were the new Israel's nucleus.

Simon Peter was both first in the list and foremost in leadership among the twelve. He and his brother Andrew were fishermen. So were James and John, the sons of Zebedee. Philip and Bartholomew were also among the twelve. Matthew is identified in this list as a tax collector. The other Gospel writers do not mention Matthew's occupation in their listings of the apostles. The mention of his disreputable former occupation may be evidence that Matthew himself was the writer here.

Alphaeus' son James and Thaddaeus were two other of the disciples. Simon the Cananaean was likely a Zealot, one of the nationalists who wanted to overthrow Roman rule by force. Last in the list is Judas Iscariot, who may also have been a Zealot. He was the disciple who later betrayed Jesus. His second name may indicate that he came from Kerioth, a Judean village. It is likely that Judas was the only non-Galilean among the twelve.

These men do not seem to be the kind we would have chosen for such an important task. But Jesus relied on them to be the first of his laborers who would begin harvesting the world's field for God.

The Apostles' Assignment (10:5-15)

Jesus sent the twelve out on a special mission. According to Mark's Gospel, he sent them out in pairs. That two-by-two arrangement may be reflected in Matthew's listing of the disciples in pairs (10:2-4).

Jesus himself could not visit all the towns and villages of Galilee in the time available to him. So he multiplied his work by sending out his disciples as his representatives. Jesus' instructions to the apostles here were specifically for this mission and not for all future Christian missions. He told the twelve to concentrate their work on "the lost sheep of the house of Israel" (v. 6). Israel's people were as sinful and as much in need of salvation as Gentiles were.

On this particular mission, the apostles were not to go to Syria, the Decapolis, or Samaria. The Jews were to have first chance at hearing that the long-awaited Kingdom was breaking into the world in the person of Jesus.

The apostles were to do the same work Jesus had been doing. They were to preach that God's kingdom was at hand. They were to heal diseases, bring the dead back to life, make the lepers clean once more, and cast demons from those possessed by them. These acts would all be signs that God's rule was becoming a reality. The power to preach and heal had been freely given to the apostles. Therefore, they were not to charge for any preaching or healing they might do.

The apostles were to travel light, taking only the necessities. This was an urgent mission trip, and the apostles needed to remain unencumbered and to put their trust in God alone. They were not to take money with them but instead were to depend upon the hospitality of those who received their message.

When first entering a village, the apostles were to inquire about a worthy home in which they might stay. They were then to stay in that home until their departure. A "worthy" (v. 13) household which would receive them and their message would be receiving the peace of the one they represented. One which rejected them would also be rejecting Jesus.

If a household or town refused to listen to them or to receive them, the apostles were to "shake off the dust" (v. 14) from their feet upon leaving. That gesture was used by Jews upon leaving Gentile lands, which they considered unclean. The Jews who refused to receive the gospel or its messengers were, Jesus was saying, as unclean as the Gentiles they labeled as being unclean.

In fact, the unreceptive towns and people of Galilee would be held to have greater guilt in the time of judgment than ancient Sodom and Gomorrah, known for their wickedness. The Galileans had the greater knowledge and privilege. Theirs, then, would be the greater responsibility and guilt.

Warnings and Assurances About Persecution (10:16-33)

Jesus declared that he was sending the apostles "out as sheep in the midst of wolves" (v. 16). They would be vulnerable as he was vulnerable. So he advised them to "be wise as serpents and innocent as doves" (v. 16). In other words, they were to use good judgment and common sense but were also to be completely sincere.

Jesus foresaw the time when his disciples would face great persecution because of their loyalty to him. That persecution did not occur on this special mission but did become a reality after Jesus' death and resurrection.

Jesus told his disciples that they might face any of three kinds of court trials. They might be tried in synagogues before the local Jewish councils, which had the authority to flog a prisoner with thirty-nine stripes. Governors, perhaps men representing Rome, would hear some of their cases. So would kings like Herod Antipas. These trials would be an opportunity to bear witness for Christ. Later on, such persecutions would be an opportunity for giving testimony to the Gentiles.

The disciples were not to worry about what to say in the hour of their trial. God's Spirit would speak through them the words they should say.

Yet another type of persecution would confront some of Jesus' disciples in the future. Family members would turn against others of the family because of their faith. Non-Christians would turn Christian family members over to the authorities. It would seem that everyone hated the disciples because of their loyalty and commitment to Jesus.

Verses 22 and 23 contain two of Jesus' most difficult sayings. Their meanings are not completely certain. In one of these sayings, Jesus assured his disciples that "he who endures to the end will be saved" (v. 22). He could have meant that a person faced with dying for Christ or denying him would be vindicated by God if he chose to be loyal unto death. Denying Jesus under such circumstances would indicate a lack of saving faith.

Some of Jesus' disciples would face possible death because of their faith in him. But they were to avoid persecution if possible. When persecuted in one place, they were to "flee to the next" (v. 23).

Another of Jesus' difficult sayings appears at this point. He told his disciples that they would "not have gone through all the towns of Israel, before the Son of man comes" (v. 23). Jesus may have been referring to something other than the final appearing of the Son of man at the end time. The transfiguration is one possibility. Or, he may have been speaking of the times he would appear after his resurrection.

Jesus told his disciples that they could not expect to receive better treatment from the world than he had received. If his enemies were calling him "Beelzebul" (v. 25; a name for Satan), they would make even stronger accusations against his disciples.

The disciples were not to fear their persecutors. Whatever the verdicts rendered about them might be, the truth would some day be known. So they should not hesitate to proclaim "in the light" (v. 27) the things Jesus had taught them in secret.

The disciples were to fear only God. Their earthly persecutors could kill their bodies but could not kill their enduring selves, their souls. God, in contrast, could "destroy both soul and body in hell" (v. 28).

Jesus gave his disciples more assurances. God, their Father, had counted even the hairs of their head (v. 30). The disciples, then, were of great value to God. Those who would acknowledge Jesus before others would receive acknowledgment by Jesus to the Father. However, Jesus would not acknowledge to the Father those who denied him before others.

More About the Cost of Discipleship (10:34-39)

Jesus had come to earth to reconcile man to God and man to man. In that sense, his purpose had been to bring peace. Divided relationships, however, often resulted when a person committed his life to Jesus. In that sense, Jesus had brought a sword rather than peace (v. 34).

Verses 35 and 36 repeat the thought of verse 21. A person's own family members might become his enemies if the following of Jesus became his life goal.

The problem came when a person had to make a choice between his family and Jesus. Jesus declared that anyone who loved a family member—for example, father, mother, son, or daughter—more than he or she loved Jesus was not worthy of Jesus. Jesus had to take first place in the life of a follower. He could claim such a priority of commitment only because love for him was the same as love for God.

Jesus went on to say that anyone who would "not take his cross and follow" him was not worthy of him (v. 38). A person condemned to death by crucifixion had to carry his own crossbeam to the execu-

tion site. To carry one's cross, then, means a willingness to die for
Jesus. Jesus was on the way to a cross, and his followers had to be
ready to share his death if necessary.

Some followers of Jesus, when faced with persecution or the pull
of other loyalties, would deny him. It would seem that in their
denial they had found life. Such apparent finding of life, however,
would result in the loss of real life. God would assure the future of
those who were willing to give up their self-will even to the point of
dying for Jesus.

Rewards for Welcoming God's Messengers (10:40 to 11:1)

The apostles were going out on this mission, and future ones, as
representatives of Jesus. People's reception of them, then, would
correspond to their reception of Jesus. Those who received (v. 40) the
apostles would be receiving Jesus and his Father.

Those who received any Christian messenger would be rewarded.
Even the minimum in hospitality, "a cup of cold water" given "to
one of these little ones" because of his or her discipleship would have
its reward (v. 42).

Remember that Jesus' disciples were going out into a world which
was, for the most part, hostile to them and their message. It would
take courage for people to receive and help them. These people
would be risking hatred themselves. But any good done to the messengers would be considered by Jesus as done to him.

Jesus' instructions to the twelve apostles concerning their mission
was now finished. Jesus went on to do more preaching and teaching
in the cities of Galilee (11:1).

Questions and Answers/Teachings
and Accusations
11:2 to 12:50

A Question from John the Baptist (11:2-6)

John the Baptist had been in prison during the entire length of
Jesus' Galilean ministry (see 4:12). According to the Jewish historian

Josephus, Herod Antipas had had John imprisoned in the fortress of Machaerus, near the Dead Sea.

There in prison, John had received some information about Jesus' ministry. But the news he heard had puzzled rather than reassured him. He had expected the Messiah to bring final judgment and overthrow all evil, but Jesus was not fulfilling that role. Evil seemed to be continuing unabated.

John sent some of his disciples to question Jesus about his identity. The disciples asked Jesus whether he actually was the Messiah ("he who is to come," v. 3) or whether they should keep looking for the Messiah. John must have felt he might have been wrong in believing Jesus to be far more than a prophet.

Jesus answered by describing his actions and told John's disciples to tell John about them. The blind had received sight. Now many who were lame could walk. He had made lepers clean and had given hearing to the deaf. Even the dead had been raised. He had preached the good news to the poor. All but two of these were signs prophesied by Isaiah (see Isa. 35:5-6; 61:1). The cleansing of lepers and the raising of the dead went even beyond Isaiah's prophecy. All of these were ways in which Jesus was bringing about the defeat of evil. They were signs of the coming of God's kingdom.

John, as well as many others, had expected the rule of God to make its presence known in a different way. So Jesus gave yet another beatitude. He declared that "he who takes no offense at me" is blessed (v. 6). He was referring to those who did not fall into the sin of rejecting him because of the kind of ministry which was his. Those who would know blessedness were those who could accept a servant Messiah rather than a conquering one.

Jesus' Opinion of John the Baptist (11:7-15)

After answering the question John's disciples had asked, Jesus talked to the crowds about John. He wanted them to know the true greatness of this man. Could it be that John's newfound uncertainty about Jesus had caused some to question John's character?

Jesus asked these people what they had gone to the wilderness to see. Had they gone to see "a reed shaken by the wind?" (v. 7). Here "reed" would mean a weak, changeable man. Of course, they had not. Had they gone to see someone dressed in finery? If so, they should have looked in a palace rather than in the wilderness.

Had they gone to see a prophet? If so, a prophet (and even more) was what they had found. For John was the messenger God had promised through the prophet Isaiah. His mission had been that of preparing the way for the Messiah.

Jesus declared that no person ever born was any greater than John. However, "he who is least in the kingdom of heaven is greater than he" (v. 11). Jesus was not criticizing John in any way. He was saying that John stood at the end of an age. John had announced the coming of the new age but would not see the cross and its results. The "least in the kingdom of heaven" would be greater than John (v. 11) in their privilege of living in the light of the cross and resurrection of Jesus.

Jesus' words in verse 12 stand among the most difficult in all the Bible to interpret. Jesus said, "From the days of John the Baptist until now the kingdom of heaven has suffered violence, and men of violence take it by force." Jesus may well have meant that from the time of John's first proclamation of the kingdom's nearness, men had been at work to defeat the kingdom. John himself had been put in prison and would become a martyr. And soon violent men would carry out a plot to kill Jesus himself.

Other interpretations are possible. For instance, Jesus may have been saying that many people had been trying to force the kingdom to fit their own conception of what it should be. Or, he could have been declaring that the kingdom of heaven had come in mightily with his miracles and exorcisms and that people had been forcibly thronging into it out of need.

Jesus went on to say that until John came, the people had the words of the Old Testament as a promise. Then John came to announce the fulfillment of "the prophets and the law" (v. 13). John was, in fact, one whose coming Malachi had prophesied (see Mal. 3:1; 4:5). John had fulfilled the role of Elijah as forerunner of the Messiah.

Jesus wanted the crowd to appreciate John's courage and importance. John's imprisonment must not keep the people from realizing the greatness of the part he had played in God's plan.

Reactions to Jesus and John the Baptist (11:16-19)

Jesus compared his own generation to children who criticized their friends for not playing games *their* way. They had played music for the "wedding" game, but their friends had not danced. They had wailed for the "funeral" game, but their friends had not joined in their mourning.

John the Baptist had lived an austere, withdrawn life as a prophet of God. He had had little social contact with others. People had criticized him for his way of life, even saying that he must be demon-possessed. In the imagery used by Jesus in this passage, John had angered the people by being unwilling to dance to their music.

Jesus, the Son of man, had been the opposite of John. His attitude toward life had been a joyful one. He had enjoyed fellowship with others. And some people, such as the religious leaders, had criticized him, even as they had criticized John. They could not understand why Jesus refused to play the "funeral" game they were demanding that he play. They exaggeratedly called him "a glutton and a drunkard" (v. 19). They were especially enraged by his friendship with religious outcasts, the sinners and the tax collectors.

Neither Jesus nor John could ever have suited these people. These two simply did not fit the mold of what many people expected the Messiah and his forerunner to be like. Yet, Jesus said, "wisdom is justified by her deeds" (v. 19). Both John and Jesus were necessary to God's plan. It was necessary for John to bring people to see their need for repentance and the reality of the coming judgment. It was equally necessary for Jesus to take the message of salvation to those who had come to realize their need. The wisdom of God in acting through John and Jesus was vindicated by the results. Through these men many had found new life.

Judgment on Unbelieving Towns (11:20-24)

John the Baptist had found it difficult to accept Jesus as primarily a servant Messiah rather than an avenging judge of evil. But Jesus went on to show that judgment as well as service was part of his role. He condemned the cities which had rejected him.

Chorazin and Bethsaida were Galilean cities near the Sea of Galilee. In them, Jesus had performed many miracles. Crowds had gathered to see these mighty works. Yet, for the most part, the people of those cities had not repented. The fact that Jesus spoke of Bethsaida and Chorazin reminds us how small our knowledge is of the extent of Jesus' Galilean ministry. The New Testament record tells us little of his ministry in those towns.

Jesus' words "Woe to you" (v. 21), addressed to Chorazin and Bethsaida, express Jesus' sorrow rather than anger or vengeance. "Alas for you" might better give the sense of his meaning here.

Jesus declared that the wicked cities of Tyre and Sidon "would have repented long ago in sackcloth and ashes" (v. 21) if they had seen Jesus' works. Tyre and Sidon would, in fact, be shown greater mercy on the day of judgment than Bethsaida and Chorazin would. They had not had the privilege of knowing Jesus and seeing his works. The accountability of the cities of Galilee was therefore greater than that of Tyre and Sidon.

Jesus had special words of condemnation for Capernaum, where he had lived during his Galilean ministry. He used words from Isaiah, originally spoken about Babylon, to say that this prosperous city, thinking it deserved rewards from God, would instead "be brought down to Hades," the realm of the dead (v. 23; see Isa. 14:13-15). Jesus declared that if the ancient city of Sodom, destroyed for its wickedness, had seen his works, it would have still been standing. Sodom would fare better in the judgment than Capernaum would.

An Invitation from Jesus (11:25-30)

Jesus closed this time of speaking to the crowd with three important statements.

The mystery of God's revelation (11:25-26).—Jesus had just spoken of his lack of success in bringing the Galilean cities to repentance. Now he thanked his Father that the truths about himself and the kingdom were revealed to "babes" while they were hidden from "the wise" (v. 25). Those who had repented, the "babes," were those humble people who were open to God and able to see him at work in Jesus. "The wise" were people like the scribes and Pharisees who felt secure in their own knowledge and so failed to see God revealed in Jesus.

The source of Jesus' authority (11:27).—Jesus declared that his Father had delivered "all things" to him (v. 27). God, then, was the source of his authority. During all Jesus' earthly life, only God the Father really knew and understood him. His own disciples, as well as his enemies, often misunderstood him. Likewise, only Jesus the Son completely knows the Father, though he reveals the Father to others.

The invitation (11:28-30).—Jesus invited those "who labor and are heavy laden" to come to him (v. 28). He would give them rest. This invitation was to those who were burdened by trying to win God's favor by keeping the law and all the elaborate scribal interpretations of it. Jesus promised relief to those burdened people who would come to him.

The Jews referred to the law as a yoke. And that yoke was a heavy one. Jesus, too, offered a yoke. But his yoke was the light one of discipleship. His disciples were to follow him and his way of life, the way of total dependence upon God. Then, with this easy yoke and light burden, their souls would know rest.

This rest would not be that of a life free of effort or sorrow. Jesus' own earthly life had its share of hard work, disappointments, and defeats. The rest he offered came from the security of knowing acceptance by God. It meant peace in the midst of life's trials and struggles.

"Reaping" and "Threshing" on the Sabbath (12:1-8)

On a sabbath day, Jesus and his disciples passed through a grainfield. Being hungry, the disciples plucked and ate some of the grain. The Jewish law allowed a person to pluck grain from another's field by hand but not with a sickle (see Deut. 23:25).

The Pharisees saw what the disciples had done and reminded Jesus that their action went against the law. The problem lay in the fact that the disciples had plucked the grain on the sabbath. The Jewish tradition contained a list of thirty-nine kinds of work which should not be done on the sabbath. The disciples had just performed at least two of these activities. Nit-picking as it sounds, they had "reaped" when they had plucked the grain. And they had "threshed" by rubbing off the husks.

Jesus used examples from the Old Testament in his reply to the Pharisees' accusation. First, he mentioned an Old Testament story about David. The Pharisees were familiar with it, but they had not understood the lesson it taught. When hungry, David and his men had eaten the holy bread which only the priests were allowed to eat (vv. 3-4; see 1 Sam. 21:1-6). This example did not have reference to the sabbath but showed that human need was allowed to take precedence over religious regulations.

And, Jesus continued, the priests themselves violated the law every sabbath (v. 5). How? The very activities involved in offering the sabbath sacrifices in the Temple were work. Yet, they were not guilty because, in their case, the sacrifice was more important than the law forbidding work on the sabbath.

Then Jesus made an amazing statement about himself. He told the Pharisees that "something greater than the temple is here" (v. 6). God's presence was thought to reside in the Temple. But God's presence was there before them incarnate in Jesus.

Again, as in 9:13, Jesus quoted Hosea 6:6 to the Pharisees. Mercy, not sacrifice, was what God wanted, he told them (v. 7). The carrying out of rituals and traditions is worthless if love is left out.

Finally, Jesus declared, "For the Son of man is lord of the sabbath" (v. 8). As the Messiah, the inaugurator of God's new age, he had the right to reinterpret the sabbath's meaning and requirements.

Healing on the Sabbath (12:9-14)

That same sabbath, Jesus went into a synagogue. One of the men present there had "a withered hand" (v. 10). The Pharisees wanted a reason to accuse Jesus. So they used the man's presence as an excuse to ask Jesus, "Is it lawful to heal on the sabbath?" (v. 10).

The Pharisees interpreted the law as allowing healing to be done on the sabbath if a person's life were in danger. Of course, the man with the withered hand was not in danger of dying from his deformity. By waiting only a few hours, Jesus could have healed him and obeyed the sabbath law as well.

But Jesus reminded the Pharisees that their law even allowed them to rescue a sheep from a pit on the sabbath. Sheep were valuable, and so in their case an exception to the basic law forbidding sabbath work could be made.

With one statement Jesus indicted the Pharisaic scale of values. He exclaimed, "Of how much more value is a man than a sheep!" (v. 12). Doing good on the sabbath is not a violation of the law, he told them. He must have felt that failure to do good when the opportunity for good presented itself would be the far greater wrong.

Jesus told the man with the deformity to hold out his hand. When he had done so, Jesus healed him, completely restoring the deformed hand. For Jesus there could have been no better day than the sabbath to win another victory over Satan.

The Pharisees were anything but happy to see the man made well, however. For the first time in Matthew's Gospel, we are told that the Pharisees began to plot Jesus' death (v. 14). Why did Jesus' attitude toward the sabbath enrage the Pharisees so? Their power and influence came from the scrupulous keeping of the oral traditions. Jesus was a threat to all they stood for.

Jesus as Fulfillment of Prophecy (12:15-21)

Realizing that the Pharisees were plotting against him, Jesus withdrew. When many people followed, he healed them. But he told them not to make public the news of their healing. Jesus did not want to unnecessarily provoke the Pharisees' further hostility, since his work was as yet far from completed. In addition, he did not want the miracle-working aspect of his ministry to be foremost in people's minds.

At this point, Matthew quoted a passage from Isaiah to show that Jesus was the prophesied Servant of the Lord (see Isa. 42:1-4).

The passage declared that the servant was one of God's own choosing, and God was pleased with this beloved one. God's Spirit was in the servant. Moreover, the servant would "proclaim justice to the Gentiles" (v. 18). Nations other than Israel would know his judgment and salvation.

The servant's ministry would be a gentle and quiet one. He would deal mercifully with those who were crushed and bruised by the world. In the end, he would bring "justice to victory" (v. 20). The goal of his ministry would be positive rather than negative. Gentiles, the people of other nations, would find their hope in him (v. 21).

The Unpardonable Sin (12:22-37)

When "a blind and dumb demoniac was brought to him" (v. 22), Jesus gave the man sight and speech. The people who saw this miracle asked in amazement whether Jesus might really be the expected Messiah, "the Son of David" (v. 23).

The Pharisees could not deny that Jesus had done a good thing in healing the man. So they attacked the source of his authority. They declared that Jesus got his power to cast out demons from Satan (Beelzebul), "the prince of demons" (v. 24).

Jesus immediately refuted this accusation. If Satan, the prince of demons, was casting out demons, then a civil war was raging in the kingdom of evil. No house or city could stand divided against itself.

In addition, Jesus reminded the Pharisees that their own disciples sometimes cast out demons. If Jesus cast out demons by Satan's power, by whose power did these "sons" of the Pharisees cast them out (v. 27)?

But if Jesus were casting out demons by God's Spirit, this was a sign that God's kingdom had come into the world. Jesus used a little parable to demonstrate the fact that his miracles were a plundering of Satan's domain. No one, he said, could "enter a strong man's house" (v. 29) and steal his possessions until the strong man had been bound. Jesus' miracles showed his power over Satan.

Jesus had come to gather together God's flock. Anyone who was not with him in this effort was against him and was guilty of helping to scatter God's flock (v. 30). There could be no neutrality with regard to Jesus.

Jesus went on to tell the Pharisees that there was only one sin for which there was no forgiveness. Criticism of Jesus could be forgiven. But "the blasphemy against the Spirit" (v. 31) could not be forgiven.

What is this blasphemy? It is calling evil good and good evil. The prophet Isaiah had condemned this state of mind long before (see Isa. 5:20). God is always willing to forgive. But a person who has received God's revelation may willfully close his mind to it and claim it has come from Satan. As long as he stays in that frame of mind, he is not open to receiving God's forgiveness.

The Pharisees were saying that Jesus' healing of the man was good fruit which had come from a bad tree. But Jesus declared that "the tree is known by its fruit" (v. 33). Good fruit can only come from a good tree.

In contrast, the Pharisees' words showed that they were evil, a "brood of vipers" (v. 34). A good man's words are good. They come from the good treasure in his heart, Jesus taught (v. 35). An evil man's words, likewise, come from his heart's evil treasure (v. 35).

Jesus warned the Pharisees that they would be judged "for every careless word" they said (v. 36). Their words would either justify or condemn them at the time of judgment.

The Demand for a Sign (12:38-45)

Some scribes and Pharisees asked Jesus to show them a sign as proof of his identity. Evidently they wanted to see some spectacular miracle, one greater than those they had already seen. But Jesus refused to use such a sign as a means of inspiring faith (see 4:5-7).

Jesus saw their demand as evidence of their unfaithfulness to God. They weren't willing to trust God to reveal himself in his own way and in his own time.

Jesus told them that they would receive only one such sign, and it would not come on their demand. That sign would be "the sign of the prophet Jonah" (v. 39). Just as Jonah spent three days and nights inside a whale, Jesus would spend three days and nights in the realm of the dead before coming forth from death, as Jonah had emerged from the whale (v. 40).

Jesus declared that the inhabitants of Nineveh would condemn his generation at the judgment. After all, they had believed Jonah's reluctant preaching, and because of their repentance, Nineveh had been spared (v. 41).

Another would also condemn his generation at the time of judgment. The queen of Sheba in Solomon's time ("queen of the South," v. 42) had traveled far to verify what she had heard of Solomon's greatness and wisdom. When she had seen and heard for herself, she believed (see 1 Kings 10:1-13). Jesus solemnly told his hearers, "behold, something greater than Solomon is here" (v. 42). Yet the scribes and Pharisees had refused to see and believe that God was at work in Jesus.

Jesus used another little parable to show what had happened to his generation. Using the popular thought of his day, he told them that when a demon, an unclean spirit, has left a person, he wanders through the desert (thought to be an abode of demons) looking for rest. Finding none, he decides to return to the man who served as his original home. He finds his old home "empty, swept, and put in order" (v. 44). Nothing has taken his place. So he goes and brings seven demons worse than himself to live there with him. The man's condition then becomes worse than it was before.

Reforms had swept Israel clean of the old outward forms of idolatry. The scribes and Pharisees had worked hard to keep it clean-swept by multiplying religious rules and regulations. But they had failed to allow God's Spirit to fill Israel's religious life. So new forms of idolatry had crept in until the true God went unrecognized when he revealed himself to them.

Jesus' True Family (12:46-50)

Before Jesus had finished speaking, his brothers and mother came to the place where he was. They stayed outside but sent in a message asking to speak to Jesus. Matthew did not mention their reason for wanting to see him. No doubt they were concerned about his safety because of his controversy with the Pharisees. We know from Mark 3:21 that Jesus' own friends "went out to seize him," thinking he was "beside himself."

Jesus' reply to the messenger was a question, "Who is my mother, and who are my brothers?" (v. 48). With his hand reaching in his disciples' direction, Jesus declared that they were his brothers and his mother. All those who did God's will were members of his true family.

Jesus was willing to put God's will above the will of his much-loved family. He could not do less than he required his disciples to do (see 10:34-39). Before his death and resurrection, Jesus' relationship with his earthly family must have been a strained one, marked by their misunderstanding of him. Later, however, his mother and brothers did become believers.

Parables About God's Kingdom
13:1-52

The Parable of the Soils (13:1-9)

Many who heard Jesus' dynamic teaching must have wondered why he was not universally acclaimed as the Messiah. Jesus answered that question and gave a challenge to his hearers in his parable of the soils. This parable is usually called the parable of the sower, but its point lies in the kinds of soil rather than in the role of the sower.

The setting (13:1-3).—Leaving the house where he was staying, Jesus sat down at the seaside. But soon the crowd became so great that he had to sit in a boat and teach from it while the crowd remained "on the beach" (v. 2). Matthew wrote that Jesus taught the crowd "many things in parables" (v. 3). Up to this point in Matthew's account, Jesus had used several very short parables. But from this point on, his use of parables became more frequent, and the parables themselves were often longer and more detailed.

The parable (13:3-8).—Jesus told the crowd a parable about a farmer who sowed his field. Farmers scattered the seed by hand as they walked over the field. Jesus declared that the sower's seed fell on four different kinds of soil. Some of the seed fell on the hard pathways in the field. Birds came and ate that seed. Other seed fell on soil which only thinly covered a layer of rock. Warmth caused those seeds to germinate quickly. But the sun caused the seedlings to wither and die, since they could not take root. Some seed fell into deeper soil which contained thorns. The seeds grew for a while, but the thorns soon choked them out.

Fortunately, some of the seed fell on really good soil. Those seeds grew, and the harvest of grain was abundant. Even the good soil had varying capacities for increase—anywhere from thirtyfold to a hundredfold. But all the good soil did bring forth a harvest.

The challenge (13:9).—Jesus ended this parable with a challenge to those who heard him: "He who has ears, let him hear" (v. 9). He was telling the crowd to be like the good soil, letting the seed of the gospel produce an abundant harvest in them. The seed of the gospel was good seed, but many people were unable to let that gospel seed take root in their lives. Later, Jesus would explain the parable to his disciples (see 13:18-23).

Jesus' Reason for Teaching in Parables (13:10-17)

The disciples asked Jesus why he spoke to the crowds in parables. Jesus' answer is difficult to interpret. We know he was *not* saying that his use of parables was for the purpose of concealing the truth from people. Yet some commentators have interpreted these verses that way.

Jesus told the disciples that because of their receptivity, they had been able "to know the secrets of the kingdom of heaven" (v. 11). The crowds, for the most part, had lacked this receptivity. Those who were already receptive would be given increased understanding. Those who were already closed to the truth would become even more blind and deaf to it.

Jesus declared that he spoke in parables to the crowds because though they heard, they didn't really understand what they heard. And though they saw, they didn't understand what they were seeing. In fact, they fit the description of the Israelites of Isaiah's day (vv. 14-15; see Isa. 6:9-10). Through parables, Jesus was trying to reach them for God. If God had not revealed himself to the people in Jesus, they would have had no chance to know him. But the choice of whether to be open to God's truth or to reject it was theirs.

Jesus went on to call his disciples "blessed" (v. 16). Why? This was true because their eyes really saw and their ears really heard. They were responsive to his truth. They were seeing and hearing the things generations of righteous people and prophets had unavailingly longed to see and hear (v. 17).

The Meaning of the Parable of the Soils (13:18-23)

Jesus went on to explain to his disciples the meaning of the parable of the soils (see vv. 1-9). His interpretation of this parable helped them understand the responses their own "sowing" of the gospel would receive.

Jesus taught that the seeds snatched from the pathway by birds corresponded to the case of those people who heard "the word of the kingdom" (v. 19) without understanding it. The devil snatched away these seeds of the gospel which had been sown in hearts closed to the truth.

The seeds sown in the thin soil which lay above rock represented the situation of some who joyfully received the word. But their discipleship lacked deep commitment. When it began to bring problems such as persecution, these fell away.

The fate of the seeds sown in thorny soil corresponded to the experience of those people who let "the cares of the world and the delight in riches" (v. 22) choke out the word sown in their hearts.

The seeds sown in the good soil represented what happened to those who heard the word of the gospel, received it, and let it grow. These bore fruit in varying amounts. Yet in every case the yield of these seeds must have exceeded the sower's expectations.

Jesus was telling his disciples that the "sowing" of the word was their responsibility. The response would be determined by the kind of "soil" on which the word fell. It was assured, however, that an abundant harvest would result from their work.

The Parable of the Weeds (13:24-30)

Jesus next told another parable in which seed was also sown. In this case, a man sowed his field with good seed. During the night, however, "his enemy came and sowed weeds among the wheat" (v. 25).

These weeds seem to have been a kind of darnel which looked like wheat until the grain appeared. When it became obvious that these weeds were mixed in with the wheat, the owner's servants went to him. They asked if he wanted them to "weed" the field, separating the darnel from the wheat.

But the patient owner decided not to risk pulling up the darnel before harvest time, since some of the wheat might be lost along with the weeds. At the time of harvest he would have the reapers gather and burn the darnel first. The wheat would be stored in the barn. Jesus would later explain this parable's meaning to his disciples (see 13:36-43).

The Mustard Seed and the Leaven (13:31-33)

Jesus then told a pair of parables about the growth of God's kingdom. The kingdom's beginnings on earth seemed small and insignificant, not at all what the Jews were expecting. How could any great outcome be expected from the ministry of a poor Galilean carpenter and his small group of followers? But Jesus declared that the end result would be totally out of proportion to the beginning.

He first compared God's kingdom to what happens when a tiny mustard seed ("the smallest of all seeds," v. 32) is sown. That little seed grows into a tree-like plant, sometimes as much as ten feet tall—large enough for birds to nest in its branches.

Jesus then compared God's kingdom to what happens when a little leaven is added to a batch of meal. He spoke of "three measures of flour" (v. 33), enough to make about forty pounds of bread. Only a small amount of leaven was needed to make the dough rise.

The increase in size brought about by the leaven was one point

Jesus was making. But he must have also been thinking about how the leaven works. The hidden leaven works from within, penetrating and transforming the dough.

God's kingdom had not come in the dramatic and outwardly powerful way people were expecting. But Jesus brought assurance that its small beginnings would lead to unbelievably great results. And he taught that, like leaven, the kingdom would be an unseen but powerful force working within the world to bring about transformation.

The Purpose of Jesus' Parables (13:34-35)

Matthew noted that at this particular time Jesus used only parables to teach the people. Jesus' use of parables fulfilled Psalm 78:2. According to this Scripture, his purpose in using parables was to reveal "what has been hidden since the foundation of the world" (v. 35). God's long-concealed purposes were now being proclaimed.

The Meaning of the Parable of the Weeds (13:36-43)

Leaving the crowds, Jesus entered the house where he was staying. At this time his disciples asked him to explain the meaning of the parable of the weeds (see 13:24-30).

Jesus told them that he himself was the sower of the good seed. The field in the parable was the world (not the kingdom or the church). The good seed represented "the sons of the kingdom," while the weeds stood for the devil's children (v. 38). The enemy, the sower of the bad seed, was the devil. The harvest was the judgment time, the end of the age. The reapers were God's angels.

The fate of the wicked at the end time would be the same as that of the weeds at harvest time. Both would face separation and fire. But "the righteous" would know life in God's kingdom, where they "will shine like the sun" (v. 43).

Why did Jesus tell this parable? It is possible that some people (such as the Pharisees) had been asking why sinners had not already been separated from the righteous, if God's kingdom had really come in the person of Jesus.

Or, the parable may have arisen from Jesus' own knowledge that not all who followed him were genuine believers. Jesus' teaching was that the job of separating the true from the false belongs to God. His disciples are not to make this judgment. For God, in his patience, is letting the true and the false remain together until the time of judgment.

The Hidden Treasure and the Pearl (13:44-46)

In two similar parables, Jesus stressed both the value and the cost of living under God's rule. These parables called Jesus' hearers to decision.

Jesus first told of a man who, by accident, discovered a "treasure hidden in a field" (v. 44). The man covered up the newfound treasure and joyfully went to sell everything he had so that he could buy the field and so own the treasure it contained. The man's joy is the most important element of the parable. He did not consider it a sacrifice to sell all he possessed, since the treasure would then be his.

Jesus' second little parable on this subject concerned a pearl merchant. After a long search for beautiful and valuable pearls, this merchant found one which surpassed all the rest. He then sold all that he owned in order to buy the valuable pearl.

Note that the first man made his joyful discovery by accident. The other made his after a long search. Perhaps Jesus was acknowledging that people come into the kingdom in different ways.

Jesus was using these parables to call his hearers to make a choice. He was offering them the chance to live under God's rule. Did they consider that opportunity worth the glad surrender of everything else?

The Parable of the Net (13:47-50)

Jesus had called his disciples to be "fishers of men" (see 4:19). These men must have asked Jesus who should receive the message they had to give. Should they carefully select those to whom they would preach the good news?

Jesus told a parable which would have answered this question. In many ways it is similar to his parable of the weeds.

This parable concerned a net (a seine) used in fishing. Two boats could pull a seine between them, or one boat could use ropes to pull the seine.

Jesus reminded his hearers how a seine, when thrown in the water, gathers in all kinds of fish. Then the fishermen sit on the shore, separating the good fish from the bad. For Jews, "bad" fish would have been those which were inedible according to Jewish law.

Jews could eat only fish with scales and fins.

Jesus declared that the situation at the end time would be like that. God's angels would separate the righteous from the evil, sending the evil to "the furnace of fire" (v. 50).

Jesus was telling his disciples that they should proclaim the gospel to all kinds of people. Inevitably, some false followers would be gathered in. But proclamation, not judgment, was the disciples' job. Judgment was certain but could wait until the end time.

The New and the Old (13:51-52)

Jesus asked his disciples whether they had understood all these teachings about the kingdom. They assured him that they had.

Then Jesus gave them another little parable to describe the kind of disciples they should be. He spoke of "every scribe who has been trained for the kingdom of heaven" (v. 52). He was likely not speaking of the scribes who were the teachers of the law. Instead, he was speaking of his disciples.

He compared these disciples he had instructed to "a householder who brings out of his treasure what is new and what is old" (v. 52). A householder would use both his old and new possessions and goods to care for the needs of his family and guests.

So too, Jesus' disciples would combine their knowledge of God's past revelation in the Old Testament with their growing knowledge of his fuller new revelation in Jesus. Only by relating the old to the new could they meet the needs of those to whom they would minister.

Controversy, Miracles, and Important Events
13:53 to 17:27

Rejection in His Own Hometown (13:53-58)

The headquarters for Jesus' ministry in Galilee had been Capernaum. But he returned briefly to his hometown, Nazareth. There he taught in the local synagogue.

Those residents of Nazareth who heard Jesus were amazed at his teaching. Already they had heard about the miracles he had done elsewhere. Now they wondered about the source of his power and wisdom.

The people of Nazareth were just too familiar with Jesus to believe he could be anyone out of the ordinary. They knew him as the son of Joseph, the carpenter. Jesus, his mother, brothers, and sisters had been their neighbors for many years. How dare he claim to be different! Surely God could not act through someone so well known to them. Matthew wrote that "they took offense at him" (v. 57). Luke included in his account of this incident the fact that the people of Nazareth actually tried to kill Jesus (see Luke 4:28-30).

Jesus found curiosity, jealousy, and outright hatred in Nazareth. But he found very little faith there. He reminded the people about the proverb which declared that a prophet receives honor everywhere "except in his own country and in his own house" (v. 57). Because there was so little faith in Nazareth, Jesus did not do there the mighty works he had done in other places. Jesus must have been deeply saddened at this rejection by the people of his own hometown.

The Death of John the Baptist (14:1-12)

Herod Antipas, a son of Herod the Great, was the tetrarch of Galilee and Perea from 4 BC until AD 39. At this time, news of Jesus' fame reached Herod. Herod's guilty conscience caused him to think that perhaps in Jesus, John the Baptist had returned from the dead to trouble him. At least what he heard about Jesus' preaching must have reminded him of John.

Herod's guilty fear came from the fact that he had been responsible for the death of John the Baptist. Herod had imprisoned John because of John's denunciation of his marriage to Herodias. Herod had been married to the daughter of the king of Nabatea. But while visiting Rome, he had fallen in love with Herodias, his brother's wife. Divorcing his own wife, he had married Herodias.

John the Baptist had openly criticized this marriage as being not a lawful marriage at all, but adultery. Note that Matthew did not call Herodias Herod's wife. Instead, Matthew, realizing that in God's eyes their marriage was not a legitimate one, referred to Herodias as Herod's "brother Philip's wife" (v. 3).

Herod would gladly have put John to death to silence him, but fear of the people kept him from doing so at first. The people, after all, considered John a prophet.

But at Herod's birthday banquet, Herodias finally succeeded in bringing about John's death. (She, too, hated John for his criticism of her marriage.) That night, Herodias' daughter danced for the probably-intoxicated Herod. Her dance pleased Herod so much that he vowed to give her anything she wanted. At her mother's urging, the girl asked for "the head of John the Baptist here on a platter" (v. 8).

Herod was fearful of publicly breaking his oath and so angering Herodias. Though still fearing the people too, he gave in to the request for John's execution.

Jewish law did not permit a person to be executed without a trial. It did not allow beheading as a form of execution, either. Yet Herod had his hated critic beheaded without any trial.

John's disciples buried John's body and went to give Jesus the sad news. Jesus' opinion of Herod Antipas was no better than that held by John the Baptist. Luke tells us of a time when Jesus referred to Herod as "that fox" (Luke 13:32). And we also know from Luke's Gospel that Jesus appeared at a hearing before Herod Antipas shortly before being crucified (see Luke 23:6-12).

The Feeding of More Than Five Thousand (14:13-21)

Upon hearing of the death of John the Baptist, Jesus went by boat "to a lonely place apart" (v. 13). No doubt he needed to be alone at this time. He may also have wanted to go beyond the jurisdiction of Herod Antipas. The crowds, however, would not leave Jesus alone. When they realized that he was crossing the Sea of Galilee, they walked around the shore to join him again.

Instead of criticizing the crowd for coming after him, Jesus "had compassion on them, and healed their sick" (v. 14). The healings, no doubt together with Jesus' teachings, so enthralled the crowd that when evening came (probably 3 PM), they were still with him. And they had not made provision for food.

The disciples, instead of asking Jesus' advice, told him to send the people to nearby villages so that they could "buy food for themselves" (v. 15). Jesus, however, had other ideas. He told the disciples to feed the crowds. The disciples told him how meager their resources were. They had available only five barley loaves and two small dried fish (v. 17), the foods eaten by the poor. In John's Gospel, this food is said to belong to a young boy (see John 6:9).

Jesus asked for the loaves and fish. Then, after the multitude had been seated on the ground, he blessed the food and broke it. He gave the pieces to the disciples to give to the people. Amazingly enough, there was plenty for all. In fact, twelve baskets of food were left over. It may be that each disciple had served from his own basket and that the baskets remained full after all had eaten. Far more food was left over than there had even been in the beginning.

Matthew noted that the crowd Jesus fed consisted of five thousand men in addition to the women and the children (v. 21). Many more than five thousand had actually been fed.

You will remember that Jesus, when tempted in the wilderness, had refused to make bread miraculously in order to satisfy his own hunger or to win followers (4:3-4). On this occasion he fed the crowds primarily because of his compassion for them. He cared about their needs.

But this miraculous feeding had other meanings as well. Moses had followed God's orders in feeding the Israelites in the wilderness (see Ex. 16). And Elisha had fed one hundred men with twenty loaves and some grain (see 2 Kings 4:42-44). This miracle was a declaration that Jesus was greater than either Moses or Elisha. Moreover, this meal had a messianic meaning, since the Jews thought of God's coming kingdom in terms of a banquet.

The importance of this miracle is underscored by the fact that of all Jesus' miracles, only this one is included in all four Gospels. Then and now the miracle assures us that whatever our needs may be, God has more than adequate resources to meet them.

Miracles on the Sea of Galilee (14:22-36)

Matthew wrote that after this miraculous feeding, Jesus "made the disciples get into the boat and go before him to the other side, while he dismissed the crowds" (v. 22). John's account of this incident sheds some light on why Jesus acted as he did.

According to John, Jesus realized that the people he had just fed were about to make him their king by force (see John 6:15). It is very likely that the disciples, with their still erroneous understanding of

Jesus' mission, had urged the crowd on. Perhaps Jesus needed to get
the disciples away from the crowd so that he could defuse the situation.

When the crowd and the disciples were gone, Jesus went to pray
by himself in the hills. After all the events of that day he must have
wanted to recommit himself to his Father's purpose and way.

Meanwhile, the disciples in their boat were battling a storm on the
Sea of Galilee. Sometime between 3:00 AM and 6:00 AM, Jesus
walked on the water to the disciples. At first the frightened disciples
thought they were seeing a ghost. But Jesus calmed their fears, saying, "it is I" (v. 27). He was literally saying, "I am." God had used
the same expression to reveal himself to Moses (see Ex. 3:14).

Peter, always impulsive, asked Jesus to bid him walk to him on the
sea. Jesus did tell Peter to come to him. At first, Peter did walk on the
water toward Jesus. But soon fear took over, and Peter began sink-
ing, crying for Jesus to save him. Jesus caught Peter but asked, "O
man of little faith, why did you doubt?" (v. 31). Peter could do anything as long as he had faith in Jesus. But when he looked away from
Jesus at his fears, he failed. Only Matthew's Gospel contains this
story of Peter's attempt to walk on the water.

The wind stopped blowing when Peter and Jesus entered the boat.
And the disciples now had the assurance they needed about Jesus.
Their understanding of his kingdom and his mission was still incom-
plete. But at this point they did worship him as the Son of God.

On the northwest side of the Sea of Galilee, they landed at Gen-
nesaret, a four-mile-long plain. There, as in other places, all those
who were sick were brought to Jesus. The faith of these sick people
may have been partly self-seeking and superstitious. They believed
they would be healed if they could only touch the fringe of Jesus'
garment (see discussion of 9:20-22). Yet even their incomplete faith
was rewarded, because Jesus cared about them. All who did touch
even his garment's fringe were healed.

Conflict with the Pharisees and Scribes (15:1-20)

A question about hand washing (15:1-9).—A group of scribes and
Pharisees came from Jerusalem to see Jesus. Doubtless they were a
delegation who had come to investigate Jesus and his work and
teachings.

These religious leaders had a question for Jesus. Why, they asked, did Jesus' disciples disobey "the tradition of the elders" (v. 2) by not washing their hands before eating? The tradition of the elders was the oral interpretation of the first five books of the Old Testament, accumulated and passed on from one generation to the next. It attempted to apply the Old Testament law to all of life. The Pharisees believed that the oral tradition was as important as the written law.

The hand washing in question here had nothing to do with hygiene. It was strictly a matter of ritual. The prescribed hand washing ritual was for the purpose of taking away any defilement which might have resulted from contact with a ritually unclean thing or person. A Gentile was one example of an "unclean" person.

The hand washing ritual practiced by these religious leaders was an elaborate one. Water jars were kept available for the mealtime washing of hands. The ritual prescribed that a certain amount of water had to be used in a certain way. Water first was poured on both hands with the fingers pointing up. Then it was poured with the fingers held downward. The fist of each hand was then used to clean the opposite hand. The strictest of the Jews practiced this hand washing between courses of a meal as well as before the meal's beginning.

Instead of directly answering the scribes' and Pharisees' question, Jesus asked the scribes and Pharisees a question of his own. He wanted to know why they had actually used their tradition as an excuse for disobeying God's commandments.

Jesus used as an example the Commandment requiring one to honor his parents (v. 4; see Ex. 20:12). Keeping that Commandment might well require material support for parents in sickness or in old age.

But the oral tradition provided a way to evade this Commandment of God. It allowed a man to say that the goods he would have used to help his parents were "corban." "Corban" could mean either "given or dedicated to God" or sworn under oath not to be used for a stated purpose. If a person said that his goods were "corban," he could not use them to aid his parents. (By the end of the first century AD, the rabbis had decided that no such vow could release a person from obligation to his parents.)

Jesus called the scribes and Pharisees hypocrites for nullifying

God's law with their tradition. He saw a perfect description of their behavior in some words of the prophet Isaiah (see Isa. 29:13). These religious leaders were giving lip service to God, but their hearts were far from him. They were teaching human tradition as God's law.

What defiles a person (15:10-20).—Speaking to the people, Jesus told them that a person is not defiled by what he puts into his mouth. In other words, defilement does not come from the outside. A person is not evil because of rituals he fails to perform or because of foods he eats. Instead, a person is defiled by "what comes out of the mouth" (v. 11).

The disciples told Jesus that his statement had offended the Pharisees. After all, the Pharisees' status with the people rested on the continuance of the oral tradition. They were respected because of their own strict observance of these rules of behavior.

Jesus told his disciples to leave the Pharisees alone. God would take care of uprooting any plant he had not planted. Jesus could have been referring to the oral law (which he did not believe to be from God) or to the Pharisees, or to both as the plant not planted by the Father.

Jesus went on to call the Pharisees "blind guides," (v. 14). They failed to see the truth of Jesus' identity and teaching. The equally blind people they led would fall with them.

Peter then, perhaps as spokesman for the disciples, asked for an explanation of Jesus' saying about what causes defilement. Marveling at their lack of understanding, Jesus explained the saying to the disciples. Putting food into the mouth simply begins the natural process of digestion. There is nothing evil in that or in eating with hands unwashed. But that which comes out of the mouth has its origin in the heart. In fact, the breaking of each of God's laws begins within a person's heart (meaning the thoughts and the will). Both evil and goodness come from within, from what a person is, not from the outside.

A Gentile Woman's Faith (15:21-28)

Going to the north of Galilee into Gentile territory, Jesus came to the area of Tyre and Sidon. Perhaps this trip was an effort to get away from the religious authorities for a time.

A woman, called a Canaanite by Matthew, came to Jesus and begged him to heal her demon-possessed daughter. Though she was a Gentile, she called Jesus "Son of David" (v. 22).

Jesus' attitude in this passage has long puzzled many Christians. At first Jesus did not even answer the distraught woman. Perhaps he wanted to hear what his disciples would say. When the disciples spoke, it was to ask Jesus to send the woman away because she was bothering them.

Jesus declared, "I was sent only to the lost sheep of the house of Israel" (v. 24). Of course, Gentiles were to be included in Jesus' mission, but the Jews needed to receive the message first. They had the best background for understanding Jesus and his message and for sharing the gospel with the world. In making the statement, Jesus may have been testing the disciples to see whether they understood that his mission reached beyond Israel. Or he may have been torn between confining his efforts to the Jews and doing all he could for Gentiles as well.

Kneeling before Jesus, the woman begged for his help. In print, Jesus' reply seems harsh to us. He told the woman it wasn't fair to throw the children's bread to the dogs. However, the word he used for dogs meant pet dogs or puppies. And it is entirely possible that Jesus was simply testing the woman's faith, speaking gently and smiling as he did so.

The woman quickly responded. Even dogs got to eat the crumbs as they fell from the table of the master, she told him. She wasn't asking for the privileges of the Jews. She simply wanted her suffering daughter to be healed.

Jesus marveled at this Gentile woman's faith. What a contrast it was to the lack of faith of the Jewish religious leaders! The woman's daughter was immediately healed.

The Feeding of More than Four Thousand (15:29-39)

Going to an area near the Sea of Galilee, Jesus went "into the hills" (v. 29). There he was thronged by a multitude who brought with them many who needed healing. When Jesus used his healing power, the mute spoke; the blind saw; the lame walked; and the maimed were made whole. Evidently this was a Gentile crowd, since "they glorified the God of Israel" (v. 31). These healings may have taken place in the area of the Decapolis, southeast of the Sea of Galilee.

After three days with Jesus, the people were hungry. The food they had brought with them was now gone. Calling his disciples to him, Jesus told them the people needed food. He felt compassion for the people and knew that without food they might faint on the journey home.

The earlier feeding of a multitude must not have taught the disciples enough about Jesus' ability to meet needs. They complained that there was no way to get enough bread for that crowd in such a deserted area.

As before, Jesus asked about the resources available. This time there were seven loaves in addition to some small fish. Taking, blessing, and breaking the food, Jesus gave it to the disciples for distribution to the seated crowd. When all had been fed, seven baskets of pieces remained. Four thousand men had been fed, not counting the women and the children.

Many have thought this story to be just a retelling of the feeding of the five thousand (see 14:13-21). However, several differences exist between the two. The first multitude was Jewish, while the second appears to have been Gentile. The numbers of loaves, fish, and baskets of leftovers are also different, as are the numbers of people fed. Even the words used for the kinds of baskets are different. The baskets which contained leftovers after the feeding of the five thousand were the narrow baskets in which Jews often carried their food. The ones used after the feeding of the four thousand were hamper-like fishermen's baskets. A short while later, Jesus would speak of the two feeding miracles as separate events (see 16:9-10). This second feeding miracle emphasized the fact that though his primary mission was to Jews, Jesus could act on behalf of the Gentiles as well.

A Demand from the Religious Authorities (16:1-12)

Earlier, some Pharisees and scribes had asked Jesus for a sign (see 12:38-39). Now Pharisees and Sadducees also "asked him to show them a sign from heaven" (v. 1), some proof of his messiahship. Their purpose in asking was to test him and so possibly diminish his influence with the people. These two religious parties differed greatly from one another but joined together to oppose Jesus.

Jesus reminded these religious leaders that they had no difficulty in interpreting what the weather would be from the color of the sky. They did not seem capable, however, of interpreting "the signs of the times" (v. 3). The Messiah was in their midst, and through him God's rule was making itself known. Yet the religious authorities of the nation were blind to all this.

Jesus refused to give the Pharisees and Sadducees a sign on demand. He declared that the only sign given to "an evil and adulterous generation" would be "the sign of Jonah" (v. 4), Jesus' own resurrection after being buried three days (see discussion of 12:38-42). Knowing that the religious leaders had no intention of believing in him, Jesus went away from them.

Jesus then went with his disciples by boat to the other side of the Sea of Galilee. Once there, the disciples realized that they had neglected to bring bread with them. So when Jesus told them to "beware of the leaven of the Pharisees and Sadducees" (v. 6), they thought he was talking about literal bread. (Leaven could refer to bread, but more often stood for evil or corrupt influence.)

Jesus was amazed that after seeing two feeding miracles, his disciples could be worried about bread. Those miracles had shown his adequacy to meet their needs. When he repeated his statement about the leaven of the Pharisees and Sadducees, the disciples finally understood. He was telling them to avoid being influenced by the teachings of these religious leaders. His teaching was enough for them.

Recognition of Jesus' Identity (16:13-20)

While Jesus was with his disciples in "the district of Caesarea Philippi," he asked them a question. Who were people saying that he, the Son of man, was? (v. 13). The disciples answered that many people were identifying Jesus with great religious figures from the past. Some were saying he was John the Baptist. Others thought he might be Elijah or a prophet like Jeremiah.

Then Jesus asked a more vital question. Who did they, his disciples, think he was? Simon answered Jesus without hesitation: "You are the Christ, the Son of the living God" (v. 16). Simon had recognized Jesus as being more than just another prophet. He had seen him as both Messiah and Son of God.

Jesus praised Simon for this confession of faith. He declared that the insight had come to Simon from God himself, not from human sources. Jesus went on to make promises which scholars have found difficult to interpret.

First, he gave Simon a new name, Peter, meaning "rock." Impulsive Simon was certainly not rocklike. But within the giving of the name was the promise of what Simon would become.

Jesus declared that "on this rock" he would build his church (v. 18). Some have thought the foundation rock of the church was to be Peter himself. The possibility that the "rock" was the faith shown by Peter in making his confession is much more likely. In a sense, that faith and the confession of it *were* to be the foundation of the church, though the church's ultimate foundation was Christ himself. Jesus promised that his church would continue to endure even in the face of "the powers of death" (v. 18).

Jesus then declared that he would give Peter "the keys of the kingdom of heaven" (v. 19). Moreover, anything Peter bound on earth would "be bound in heaven," and anything he loosed on earth would be "loosed in heaven" (v. 19). The keys symbolized authority. And only a short while later, Jesus gave this power to "bind" and "loose" to all the disciples and ultimately to his church (see 18:18). What did these terms mean?

In Aramaic the terms translated "bind" and "loose" had to do with forbidding and permitting. It seems that Jesus was giving his disciples authority to announce the gospel. One's acceptance or rejection of the gospel determined if one were loosed from sin or remained bound by sin.

This recognition of Jesus' messiahship marked an important progressive step in the disciples' understanding of Jesus. But Jesus "strictly charged" (v. 20) them not to tell anyone that he was the Messiah. He was not to be the kind of Messiah the Jews expected. Even his twelve close disciples had not yet comprehended that fact. Use of the title of Messiah at this point could lead only to misunderstanding.

The Path of Christ and His Followers (16:21-28)

After Peter had made his confession acknowledging Jesus' messiahship, Jesus began to teach his disciples what his messiahship actually involved. He would be a suffering Messiah, not a conquering military leader. He would go to Jerusalem. There the Jewish Sanhedrin (composed of scribes, elders, and chief priests) would cause him to "suffer many things" (v. 21). Finally, he would be killed but would be raised the third day.

Peter, his mind tuned in only to Jesus' words about suffering and dying, could not believe what Jesus was saying. Surely the Messiah would not have to suffer! Peter may have spoken for the entire group of disciples when he assured Jesus that these things would never happen to him.

Jesus' reaction to Peter's words was swift and severe: "Get behind me, Satan!" (v. 23), he told Peter. Jesus had used similar words to rebuff Satan during the wilderness temptations (see 4:10). Satan, like Peter, had tried to get Jesus to follow the easy way to a popular messiahship and reject the way of suffering.

A short while before, Peter had spoken words inspired by God. Now he was being used as Satan's spokesman. Jesus had called him the "rock." Now Peter had become a stumbling block to Jesus instead.

Jesus knew that his disciples would also have to follow his difficult path. He told them that being his disciple would mean self-denial, taking up one's cross, and following him (v. 24). These disciples might have to face literal physical death as Jesus' followers. At the very least they would have to be willing to suffer and die for him. They would definitely have to "die" to self-will.

Jesus taught that anyone who tried to "save" his life either by denying Christ in order to avoid physical death or by living for self instead of God would lose his true and higher life. That person would never become what God intended him to be. Paradoxically, the person who seemingly had lost his life for the sake of Christ (whether literally or by self-denial) would know real and lasting life.

The world has no lasting security to offer. Such security can come only by living one's life for God. A person might achieve great worldly success by making material prosperity or earthly power his goal. But if his true life were lost in the process, where would his profit be? After so wasting his life, nothing could be given in exchange to regain it.

Jesus' earthly life would end in suffering and death. But that seeming defeat would not really be the end. He will return in glory. And in the time of judgment, he will make payment to each person for what that individual has done on earth.

Jesus declared that some of those listening to him then would be living to see him "coming in his kingdom" (v. 28). It seems most likely that he was speaking of the events which would surround his resurrection rather than those which would be a part of his final coming at the end time.

The Transfiguration (17:1-13)

Six days after Peter's confession of Jesus' messiahship, Jesus took Peter, James, and John with him up on a high mountain (probably Mount Hermon). It may be that these three disciples had a better understanding of Jesus than the others had.

There on the mountain, these three disciples saw Jesus changed or transfigured before their very eyes. Jesus' face took on the radiance of the sun, and even his clothing "became white as light" (v. 2). For that brief moment, the disciples saw Jesus as the heavenly Lord.

As the disciples watched, Moses and Elijah appeared and spoke with Jesus (v. 3). From Luke's account, we know that their conversation with Jesus concerned his coming death (see Luke 9:31). Moses symbolized the law, while Elijah stood for the prophets. Jesus had come to fulfill both.

These two men were also connected in Old Testament writings with the age of the Messiah. Their appearance with Jesus meant in part that he was the prophet like Moses foretold in Deuteronomy 18:15 and also the Messiah whom Elijah would precede, as foreseen in Malachi 4:5.

Evidently Peter, not understanding what was happening, wanted to prolong the vision. He told Jesus that he could build booths for him and both the others. Before Peter had even stopped speaking, they were all overshadowed by a bright cloud. God spoke from the cloud as he had spoken earlier at Jesus' baptism. Again he called Jesus his "beloved Son" (v. 5) with whom he was pleased. But this time he added, with possible reference to Deuteronomy 18:15, "Listen to him" (v. 5). They were to take Jesus as their authority.

Hearing the voice of God, the awestruck disciples "fell on their faces" (v. 6). Touching them, Jesus told them to get up and stop being fearful. When they looked, the two visitors were gone. Jesus stood alone.

As they descended the mountain, Jesus told the three disciples not to tell anyone about this vision until after his resurrection. He did not want false hopes for a political messiah read into it. And as yet, the disciples' understanding of the experience was doubtless incomplete.

At this time, the three disciples asked Jesus about the scribes's teaching on the coming of Elijah before the Messiah. Jesus assured them that his "Elijah" had already come, though unrecognized as such by the religious leaders. The disciples realized that John the Baptist was the "Elijah" Jesus was speaking about.

The Disciples' Lack of Faith (17:14-21)

The overwhelming experience on the mountain soon gave way to everyday reality. A crowd had gathered with the nine remaining disciples. And at Jesus' appearance, a man came and knelt before him, begging him for help. The man's son, an epileptic, suffered from dangerous falls into fire and water. The nine disciples who had not gone with Jesus had tried without success to heal the boy. (Jesus had earlier given them the authority to heal, 10:1.)

Jesus wondered aloud how long he could bear with such a faithless generation as his disciples seemed to represent. When the boy was brought to Jesus, he received immediate healing.

The nine disciples asked Jesus why they had not been able to heal the boy. Jesus blamed their failure on their lack of faith. Even a small amount of faith (as small as the tiny mustard seed) would be sufficient to remove great obstacles, he told them. Jesus used the metaphor of moving the mountain at which they stood to stress the point that with faith in God, no obstacle is insurmountable.

More Words Foretelling Jesus' Death (17:22-23)

Jesus and his disciples gathered again in Galilee. Once more he tried to prepare them for what would happen on their coming visit to Jerusalem. He told them he would be arrested and killed. Yet on the third day he would be raised from death.

The disciples seemed not to hear his words about resurrection.

They could only feel a deep sadness because of the separation from Jesus they were soon to experience.

A Question About Taxes (17:24-27)

Of the four Gospel writers, only Matthew has given us an account of an unusual incident which took place in Capernaum. There the poll-tax collectors came to Peter and asked him whether Jesus paid the annual half-shekel tax Jewish males were required to pay for Temple upkeep. Peter answered "Yes" (v. 25), but he must have hoped to learn Jesus' real position on the matter later.

At home, Jesus spoke to Peter about the tax, using the example of kings and nations to make his point. He told Peter that kings do not tax their sons. He may have been saying that kings tax subject nations, not their own citizens. Or, more likely, he was saying that kings tax their subjects, not members of their own families. Jesus declared that as sons of God's kingdom, he and his disciples should be free from having to pay the Temple tax.

But at this point, Jesus taught an important lesson. In order not to offend the Jews he was trying to reach, he would pay the tax. He then gave instructions to Peter. Peter was to catch a fish with a hook. The first fish he would catch in that way would have in its mouth a shekel. With that shekel, Peter was to pay the tax for both Jesus and himself.

This incident has puzzled many Bible scholars, since it seems to show Jesus performing a miracle for his personal convenience. Some believe Jesus told Peter to use his occupation as a fisherman to earn enough money to pay the tax. But possibly Jesus was simply showing by this sign that he was God's all-powerful Son who had a right to be exempt from the Temple tax.

The miracle is actually not the point of this story at all. The point is that concern for others is a valid reason for not always exercising one's rights. If Jesus and his disciples had failed to pay this religious tax, others would have misunderstood. Jesus' teaching might have come into disrepute. People might have been lost to the kingdom. The loving thing to do was to take into account their influence on others and pay the tax.

Insights for Disciples
18:1 to 20:34

Greatness in the Kingdom (18:1-4)

The disciples' question (18:1).—Jesus' disciples came to him to ask a question: "Who is the greatest in the kingdom of heaven?" (v. 1). We know from Mark's Gospel that the disciples had been discussing this question among themselves (see Mark 9:33-37).

But the very asking of this question revealed a serious misunderstanding of what God's kingdom is. Evidently the disciples saw it as similar to an earthly political kingdom with a ranked power structure.

How to enter the kingdom (18:2-3).—Jesus first, in an acted parable, showed the disciples what must take place before a person can even enter the kingdom. He called a child to him and told the disciples they must "turn and become like children" (v. 3), or they would never enter God's kingdom.

By "turn" Jesus basically meant to be converted, to change life direction in terms of values and attitudes. Without that turning, a person would find it impossible to become like a child.

This turning is actually the same as the new birth about which Jesus had taught Nicodemus (see John 3:3).

A person cannot bring this new birth about by himself. It can come only from God. It provides a new beginning in which a person's whole life can become radically different. Earthly values and self-will will stop being so important to the person who has received the new birth. God's will becomes all-important.

Why did Jesus use a child as the symbol of a citizen of God's kingdom? Surely he did not mean his disciples should be childish and immature. Instead, he wanted them to be *childlike* in some ways.

A child is, first of all, dependent and realizes that he is dependent. A child cannot survive without the help and support of his parents or other adults. A citizen of God's kingdom is, likewise, dependent on God and willingly acknowledges that dependence.

A child is trusting, believing that his parents will meet his needs. A citizen of God's kingdom must also trust God to meet all his needs.

Perhaps most important, a child is humble. He realizes that he is small, and he does not try to be anything other than what he is. A citizen of God's kingdom humbly submits to God, realizes his limitations, and does not demand first place.

The greatest in the kingdom (18:4).—Jesus then answered his disciples' question about greatness in God's kingdom. The greatest person in God's kingdom would be one who "humbles himself like this child" (v. 4). Jesus' statement represented a complete reversal of the world's values. Those qualities earth counted least important would be the most important in the kingdom.

Today, we are not often concerned with the rank we will hold in God's kingdom. But we are very concerned with our status here and now on earth. Excessive ambition, greed, and love of power characterize many of our lives. Jesus counts humility as the mark of greatness.

Responsibilities Toward Little Ones (18:5-6)

Jesus identified himself with children and with those lowly people the world often ignored or rejected. To receive a child or a child in the faith (a new or immature Christian) in Jesus' name, as his representative, is to receive Jesus himself. No one is unimportant to Jesus. He wants his disciples to care for those who are weak.

But those who come in contact with "these little ones who believe in" Jesus (v. 6) have a special responsibility as far as their influence goes. They are to be careful not to lead them into sin. By nature children (and the weak) look to others for leadership and example.

Jesus stressed the seriousness of causing a weaker Christian to sin. He declared that the person who did so would be better off if a huge millstone were hung around his neck and he were drowned in the sea. The millstone of which Jesus spoke was a grinding stone so big that a donkey would have to turn it. And the body of a person drowned in the sea's depth would never be recovered for burial. Jesus was giving a vivid word picture to underline how terrible a thing it is to cause another to sin.

A person's own sin may end with himself. But if one person leads another into sin, he may have begun a chain of influence without end. What stumbling blocks may be put in another's way and lead him to sin? A proud or arrogant attitude and a bad example in conduct are just some of the obstacles which might be present in one person's life and block another's pathway to the Christian life.

What to Do About Temptation (18:7-9)

Jesus went on to teach his disciples more about the problem of temptations. He declared that it was "necessary" for temptations to come (v. 7). He meant that temptations are inevitable in the kind of world in which we live, not that God wills them. Though temptations will occur, Jesus taught that a person should be careful not to be the means by which they come to others.

But what about the temptations an individual personally faces? Jesus gave the same advice he had given in his Sermon on the Mount concerning lust (see 5:27-30). In both instances he used the analogy of radical surgery to illustrate the means for keeping sin out of one's life.

The literal severing of a limb or plucking out of an eye would, of course, do little to protect a person from sin. Jesus was talking about the kind of self-discipline which will get rid of whatever is causing a temptation to sin.

When faced with possible loss of physical life, a person will readily agree to the life-saving surgical removal of a diseased organ. So too one's spiritual life, in order to be healthy, requires radical removal of anything which will corrupt it.

The Lost Sheep (18:10-14)

Jesus warned his disciples against having contempt for "these little ones" (v. 10). Using the ideas prevalent in his day, he remarked that even the little ones, probably meaning the weaker or less mature members of the Christian flock, each had a guardian angel with constant access to the Father. He was stressing the untold value to God of every single person, no matter how lowly or unimportant that person might seem by earthly standards.

To illustrate God's love for even the weak, Jesus told a parable about a lost sheep. Luke also included this parable in his Gospel, though he placed it in a different context (see Luke 15:3-7).

Jesus' story concerned a shepherd with one hundred sheep. What would happen if just one of those sheep went astray? Jesus declared that the shepherd would not be content to have the ninety-nine safe and sound. He would leave the flock and go out and look until he had found the wandering sheep.

Where grass was sparse, sheep often wandered away to find food. And they easily got into situations from which they had to be rescued if they were to survive. A shepherd's rescue of his sheep might involve considerable time, effort, and risk to his own safety.

But, Jesus remarked, how happy the shepherd is when he finds the lost sheep! His rejoicing over it is even greater than his rejoicing over the members of the flock who did not wander away.

Jesus was painting an unforgettable verbal portrait of God here. He was showing a God who loves each individual and who will take the initiative in searching for and finding those who are lost. He was revealing the fact that the Father knows pure joy when one of his lost little ones is found. God does all he can to make certain that none of them will perish.

Discipline Within the Church (18:15-17)

In his Sermon on the Mount, Jesus had taught the necessity for making things right with a brother one had offended before bringing an offering to God (see 5:23-24). He placed responsibility on the wrongdoer for bringing about reconciliation.

In this present passage, Jesus again discussed wrong done to a brother. This time he was concerned with the effect a breach between Christians would have on the larger fellowship of the church. He described a four-step procedure for dealing with the problem of being wronged (or sinned against) by a brother. The aim of this church discipline was to be reconciliation of the brothers and restoration of the wrongdoer.

The first step in remedying the problem would be for the wronged one (not, in this case, the wrongdoer) to go to his Christian brother and confront him with what he had done. The meeting would be between the two alone, and, hopefully, reconciliation could be achieved in this way.

If the first attempt failed, the offended brother was next to take two or three others with him. (According to Deut. 19:15, no charge could be sustained without two or three witnesses.) These witnesses could observe the attitudes and motives on both sides and attempt to bring about reconciliation.

If even this second step failed, Jesus taught that the matter should be brought before the assembled church. Here again, reconciliation and restoration were to be the goals. If the church failed to bring the wrongdoer back into harmony with his brother, the procedure would be carried to the fourth step. The church would exclude the erring brother from its fellowship because of his unwillingness to overcome the barrier between himself and his brother.

That last step sounds harsh. But, by his attitude and behavior, that person had been saying all along that he was not really a part of the church's fellowship at all. The church's action of exclusion would simply be an acknowledgment of that person's own self-revealed relationship to the church.

The Authority of the Church (18:18-20)

Earlier, Jesus had promised Peter the authority to "bind" and "loose" (see 16:19). Here the church's authority seems to apply also to the right to accept and expel members. In this passage Jesus extended the promise to the entire Christian community.

Jesus told the disciples, as the nucleus of his church, that whatever they bound on earth would "be bound in heaven" (v. 18). Whatever they loosed on earth would "be loosed in heaven" (v. 18). He meant that the church's action in receiving or expelling a member would be the same as heaven's action in the case.

However, the church's action in the matter was to conform to Jesus' teaching and not be an arbitrary undertaking. The receiving or expelling of a member for superficial reasons would find no answering echo in heaven. The church is not free, for example, to receive an unbeliever into membership or to refuse membership only on the basis of social status or race. The church has the responsibility of accepting everyone who has been accepted by God already. And the church should expel only those members who have already rejected the church.

The church and its members also have the responsibility of obtaining God's guidance in decision making. Jesus promised that "if two of you agree on earth about anything they ask, it will be done for them by my Father in heaven" (v. 19). He promised to be there with any two or three who were gathered to pray in his name.

At first glance, this promise looks like a way for two people to get anything they want. That, however, was not Jesus' teaching. The phrase "in my name" (v. 20) means that those who are gathered want to find Jesus' will and are conforming their request to his nature. He is actually praying through them. So what they ask and receive will be in conformity with his will.

The Jews believed that God's divine presence was with those engaged in studying the law. Jesus promised to be that divine presence in the midst of those gathered to seek his will (v. 20).

A Parable About Forgiveness (18:21-35)

A question and an answer (18:21-22).—Peter, probably acting as spokesman for the disciples, asked Jesus how often it was necessary to forgive a brother. Would seven times not be enough (v. 21)?

Seven times may have seemed a generous number to Peter, but not to Jesus. He told Peter that he should forgive his brother "seventy times seven" (v. 22). Seventy times seven meant "without limit." The truly forgiving spirit does not keep a running account of the times it forgives. It is willing to forgive whenever a brother repents.

A parable (18:23-34).—Jesus told a parable found only in Matthew's Gospel to teach his disciples the importance of forgiveness. He began by telling about a king who decided "to settle accounts with his servants" (v. 23). One of those servants owed the king ten thousand talents (roughly the equivalent of ten million dollars) and had no possible way of repaying the debt. The king ordered the debtor and his family to be sold, along with all his possessions.

Falling to his knees, the indebted servant promised to pay all he owed if only the king would not carry out the intended punishment. The king took pity on the servant and, amazingly enough, forgave him the enormous debt.

But as he was leaving the king's presence, the servant met a fellow servant who owed him the small sum of one hundred denarii (roughly the equivalent of twenty dollars). You might think the servant would have gladly forgiven that tiny debt, since he had just been forgiven such a large one. Instead, the servant grabbed the man by the throat and demanded payment, refusing to listen to the man's pleas for mercy. He even had the man put in prison.

When the king heard what had happened, he called the first

servant to him and angrily denounced his action. He ordered the servant put in prison until his debt was paid off. And how could he ever pay the debt from prison?

The parable's application (18:35).—Jesus applied the parable to the lives of his hearers. No forgiveness they might ever show a brother could compare to the forgiveness already shown them by God. If they were not willing to forgive their brother from the heart, they would themselves find no forgiveness from God. It is not that God is unwilling to forgive. But a person with an unforgiving spirit is incapable of receiving God's forgiveness.

Teachings About Divorce (19:1-12)

Jesus left Galilee and went into "Judea beyond the Jordan" (v. 1). He healed the sick among the crowds which followed as he traveled.

The question (19:3).—At this time Pharisees asked him a question about divorce in order to test him. They asked whether it was lawful for a man to divorce his wife for any reason. Jesus had already given some teaching on this subject in his Sermon on the Mount (see discussion of 5:31-32).

In Jesus' day, the rabbinic school of Hillel held that divorce was lawful for almost any cause. According to this school, a man was even justified in divorcing his wife if she burned his dinner. The school of Shammai, in contrast, held that only the wife's adultery was a lawful reason for divorce.

Back to the beginning (19:4-6).—Jesus went back to God's purpose in creating man and woman. He quoted from Genesis 2:24 to show that God's ideal for marriage was the lasting union of a man and a woman. Man was not to dissolve this God-joined union.

Another question and answer (19:7-9).—The Pharisees countered with another question. If such was God's purpose, why had Moses stated that a husband could divorce his wife by giving her "a certificate of divorce" (v. 7; see Deut. 24:1).

Jesus told the Pharisees that this legislation of Moses had come about because of the hardness of men's hearts. (At least the certificate of divorce did give the divorced woman some protection.) But from the beginning, the time of creation, God's ideal for marriage had stood. Divorce violated that ideal.

Jesus then stated that any man who divorced his wife for any reason except adultery was committing adultery himself if he married
another woman. Jewish women in that day had few rights. They
could not divorce their husbands, though their husbands could
divorce them. It would have been both cruel and adulterous for a
husband to divorce an innocent wife to marry someone else. If the
wife had committed adultery, however, the marriage would have
already suffered a break. Jesus was protecting the position of
women, who were helpless in a male-dominated society.

The disciples' reaction and Jesus' reply (19:10-12).—The disciples
were amazed at Jesus' teaching. They declared that it might be better for a man not to marry at all if God's ideal for marriage was so
high. Jesus told them that not everyone could "receive this saying"
(v. 11). For various reasons, some men did not marry. Some, like
Jesus himself and John the Baptist, chose not to marry so that they
could devote themselves completely to the work of God's kingdom.
Jesus did not, however, elevate celibacy over marriage.

Blessing the Children (19:13-15)

Children were then brought to Jesus, probably by their mothers,
so that he could "lay his hands on them and pray" (v. 13). These
mothers had seen Jesus' healing power and must have wanted this
man's blessing for their children. The scene was a beautiful one, but
it was spoiled by the attitude of the disciples. They "rebuked the people" (v. 13), probably for interrupting Jesus' busy schedule. Perhaps
we should not be too critical of the disciples. After all, they loved
Jesus and only wanted to protect him.

Jesus overruled the disciples and invited the children to come to
him. According to Mark's account, Jesus was "indignant" at the disciples' attitude (see Mark 10:14). Had he not recently taught the disciples that the child, with his or her qualities of trust and awareness
of dependency, was the symbol of those to whom God's kingdom
belonged? (v. 14; see 18:2-4). Jesus blessed the children by laying
"his hands on them" (v. 15). Mark's account adds that "he took them
in his arms" (Mark 10:16).

This passage has been used to support the doctrine of infant baptism. However, that is an erroneous use of the passage. These verses

do teach Jesus' appreciation of the value of children and his willingness to receive them. And they commend his attitude toward children to his followers.

Demands of the Kingdom (19:16-26)

The young man's questions (19:16-22).—An individual described as a "young man" (v. 22) by Matthew and "a ruler," perhaps of the synagogue, by Luke (Luke 18:18), came and asked Jesus a question. That question was, "Teacher, what good deed must I do, to have eternal life?" (v. 16). He evidently believed that eternal life could be earned.

Jesus first told the man that only God can be described as good. There is no deed worthy enough to earn eternal life in God's kingdom. But, going along with the man's line of thought, Jesus reminded him of the commandments which God had given. Keep these commandments, Jesus told the man, and you will have the life you are looking for.

The young man wanted to limit what he had to do. So he asked Jesus which commandments he should be sure to keep. Jesus named several of the last of the Ten Commandments and gave their summary from Leviticus 19:18 as well: "You shall love your neighbor as yourself" (v. 19). These laws concerned human relationships and responsibilities.

The young man declared overconfidently that he had kept all the commandments Jesus had mentioned. He wanted to know what he still lacked. It seems that he sincerely wanted eternal life and sensed that something was missing in his life.

Jesus told him that there was one way he could achieve his goal of eternal life. He must sell all his possessions, giving the proceeds to the poor. Then he must follow Jesus.

The young man was very rich and simply could not bring himself to give up what he owned. So he sorrowfully left Jesus' presence. Jesus had put his finger directly on the young man's problem. Money had become too important in his life and stood between him and the life he wanted.

Jesus did not and does not require every one of his followers to give up all belongings in order to be his disciples. He does require the giving up of anything which stands in the way of complete discipleship.

The danger in riches (19:23-26).—Turning to his disciples, Jesus told them that the rich would find it very hard to enter God's kingdom. In fact, a camel would find it easier to go through the eye of a needle than a rich man would find it to enter into God's kingdom.

In astonishment, the disciples cried, "Who then can be saved?" (v. 25). It is likely that they considered riches a mark of God's favor. If even the rich would find salvation difficult, it seemed to them that no one could be saved.

Jesus told them that in human power alone salvation is impossible. But, he added, "with God all things are possible" (v. 26). No one, rich or poor, can enter the kingdom on his or her own merit. God's law drives every person to the knowledge of personal failings. But with God's power and mercy, the seemingly impossible can become the possible.

The Rewards for Christ's Disciples (19:27-30)

The rich young man failed to sacrifice his possessions to follow Jesus. But Jesus' twelve apostles had given up a great deal in terms of earthly security to follow him. Peter reminded Jesus of this. Then he asked what reward they would have for their sacrifices.

Jesus assured the Twelve that in the world to come they would be sharers with him in his power and his glory. His picture of the twelve sitting on thrones, "judging the twelve tribes of Israel" (v. 28), probably is not to be taken literally. Jesus was simply describing the exalted position his disciples would enjoy.

Moreover, their earthly sacrifices for Christ would seem small in comparison to the rewards they would receive. In addition to receiving eternal life, they would be repaid a hundred times over for all they had given up on earth.

Jesus ended this section with a warning. In the new world, earthly values would be reversed. Many who thought they had accomplished much and so deserved much would be surprised to find themselves last in the kingdom. And many who had assumed they would be last will, in reality, be first.

The Parable of the Vineyard Workers (20:1-16)

Jesus told a parable to illustrate the saying about the first being last and the last being first in God's kingdom (see 19:30). His story concerned a landowner who early one morning went to the marketplace to hire workers for his vineyard. He hired a group of laborers at about 6:00 AM, promising them the usual wage of a denarius for one day's work.

Around nine o'clock, seeing others who needed work standing in the marketplace, he hired yet another group. To these he promised to give "whatever is right" (v. 4). Then, at about noon and at about 3:00 PM, he hired more laborers. Finally, even at the eleventh hour, about 5:00 PM, he hired still more.

The Jewish law required that workers be paid when each workday ended. So at about 6:00 PM, the owner instructed his steward to pay the workers, beginning with those called last and ending with those called first.

Surprisingly, those who had worked only one hour received a full day's pay, just as did those who had worked long and hard for twelve hours. Those who had worked all day complained to the owner. They couldn't deny that the owner had kept his part of the bargain. He had paid them what he had promised. But they were jealous of those who had been paid as much as they after so little work. And they were angry because they hadn't received a bonus.

The owner reminded one of the complainers that since he *was* the owner, he could spend his money as he chose. And he chose to be generous with all his workers, not just with those who had worked in his vineyard all day. He would reward his workers according to need rather than by what they strictly deserved.

The main point of this parable is God's grace, by which he chooses to bless all who come to him. No doubt the scribes and Pharisees were the targets of this parable, since they had criticized Jesus for teaching that God would receive sinners. They thought that only they, who had kept the law so scrupulously for so long, deserved God's rewards. The vineyard owner in the parable could have given the last workers an amount exactly corresponding to the amount of work done. But God cannot give only a fraction of his love to those who come to him.

Note that in this parable all the workers except the first, who had an agreement with the owner, went to work in a spirit of trust. They had no bargain with the owner but believed that he would fairly compensate them without an amount being agreed upon. So, in God's kingdom, those who feel so righteous and deserving may find themselves taking second place to those who have gladly served with no thought of reward.

Jesus' Third Statement About His Death (20:17-19)

On the way to Jerusalem, Jesus once again told his disciples what would happen there. Twice before, he had tried to explain coming events to them, but they had not understood (see 16:21-23; 17:22-23).

Now Jesus told them what would happen in greater detail than before. There in Jerusalem he would be delivered up to his enemies, the scribes and chief priests. These religious leaders would "condemn him to death" (v. 18). Then they would "deliver him to the Gentiles" (v. 19), the Romans, for mockery, scourging, and execution by crucifixion. But "on the third day" (v. 19), he would be raised from death.

More About Greatness (20:20-28)

The mother of James and John came with her sons with a special request for Jesus. Kneeling before Jesus, she asked that her two sons be given special places of honor in his kingdom, one at his right hand, one at his left. It is almost certain that James and John had their mother make this request for them. If Jesus, facing the cross, had become angry at their self-seeking request, we would certainly understand. But he remained patient with them.

Jesus told these two close disciples that they really didn't know what they were asking. He had been talking about his coming death, while they were thinking about having first place in his kingdom. He asked whether they were "able to drink the cup" he was going to drink (v. 22). In other words, were they ready to die with him? The two brothers confidently answered that they were able. Obviously they still did not understand the kind of kingdom Jesus would have. But their loyalty to him at this point was commendable.

Jesus assured them that they *would* drink his cup. (James would be the first of the twelve to face martyrdom; see Acts 12:1-2. And, throughout a long life of service, John would stand ready to die for

Jesus.) However, Jesus also declared that the decision as to who would have positions of honor in his kingdom was not his to make. Only the Father himself knew who would occupy the places of honor.

The other ten of the apostles "were indignant" (v. 24) with John and James for making this request. Could it be that each of them wished he had asked first for a position of honor?

Jesus then spoke to all the disciples about the difference between earthly greatness and the greatness he asked of his followers. In the Gentile world, he told them, greatness is measured by the authority and domination one person holds over others. Jesus measured greatness far differently. To be great among his followers, a person would have to voluntarily choose to become a servant to others, a slave, giving up his own rights.

Verse 28 stands among the most valuable verses in Matthew's Gospel. In it Jesus declared that he had come to serve rather than to be served. He was the heavenly Son of man who would possess glory, dominion, and an everlasting kingdom (see Dan. 7:13-14). Yet he had come in the form of a servant, as Isaiah had prophesied.

Then, for the first time, Jesus told the disciples what the meaning of his death would be. He saw that mankind was in slavery to sin. His death by crucifixion would be the ransom needed for their liberation.

The Healing of Two Blind Men (20:29-34)

Jesus and the disciples left Jericho, followed by a large crowd. As they traveled, they came upon two blind men sitting beside the road. Hearing that Jesus was passing that way, the two men cried out to him for mercy. They used the messianic title, "Son of David" (v. 30).

The crowd tried to get the men to be quiet. We do not know why. Perhaps they feared trouble from the authorities if Jesus were publicly called Messiah. Or, it may well be that Jesus was teaching as he walked with the crowd. The shouts of the blind men may have been drowning out Jesus' words.

But Jesus heard the repeated cries of the blind men and asked what they wanted. At their request, out of compassion, he healed

them both. The men were so grateful for their healing that they
became Jesus' followers.

All through chapters 18—20, the disciples' spiritual blindness has
been apparent. The twelve did not realize how inadequate their
understanding of Jesus and his kingdom really was. At this point
Jesus found it less difficult to give physical sight to these two blind
men who had faith than to give spiritual sight to his closest followers.

Growing Conflict with the
Religious Leaders
21:1 to 23:39

Royal Entry Into Jerusalem (21:1-11)

Jesus was nearing Jerusalem and the last days of his earthly life.
He planned to make a dramatic entry into the city to make himself
known as the Messiah, but not as the kind of Messiah most people
were expecting.

The time of the feast of Passover was near, and Jerusalem would
be thronged with pilgrims from many countries. All male Jews who
lived within a twenty-mile radius of Jerusalem were required to
travel there for Passover. But many from distant places also went to
Jerusalem for this feast, which was the greatest one in the Jewish
religion.

One estimate is that two-and-one-half million Jews may have been
present in Jerusalem during a Passover celebration. Jesus could have
chosen no better time for symbolically presenting himself to the
Jews. Yet he was fully aware that the minds of the religious leaders
were already set against him. He could expect nothing but hostility
from them.

Preparation for the entry (21:1-7).—It seems that Jesus had already made plans for a donkey and her colt to be ready for him. At
Bethphage near Jerusalem, he sent two of his disciples to get the animals for him. They were to untie the donkey and colt when they

found them. If anyone questioned their action, they were to say, "The Lord has need of them" (v. 3).

If "Lord" here meant Jesus, the disciples' statement would be a kind of password telling the one in charge of the donkey and colt that Jesus had sent for them, as he had earlier arranged. But "lord" can also mean master or owner. It may be that the owner of the animals was a disciple of Jesus. In that case, the disciples would be saying that the animals' owner had agreed to their being sent.

Matthew noted that all this was in fulfillment of Zechariah 9:9. That prophecy foresaw the messianic king entering Jerusalem mounted on a donkey's colt. A warlike king would have ridden a horse. Jesus would be showing that his messiahship was spiritual instead military.

The two disciples brought the donkey and colt as Jesus had instructed them. They laid garments on the animals, and Jesus sat on the colt. According to Mark 11:2, the colt had never been ridden. That fact underlined the uniqueness and the sacredness of this event.

The crowd's response (21:8-11).—Though he was riding a donkey, the crowd gave Jesus the kind of greeting they would have given a king. Most laid garments down in his path. Others spread tree branches along the roadway. These were signs that they were honoring him.

The crowd shouted to him words from Psalm 118:26. This was one of the Hallel Psalms used to greet pilgrims who came to Jerusalem at feast times. But to this verse the crowd added the messianic title "Son of David" (v. 9), referring to Jesus. The shout of "Hosanna" (v. 9) originally meant "Save now" but here may be simply a shout of praise.

When Jesus entered the city, all of Jerusalem took note. Everyone asked who Jesus was. The crowd answered that he was Jesus the Galilean, the prophet who had come from Nazareth (v. 11). It is just possible that they were identifying Jesus as the messianic prophet like Moses the people were expecting (see Deut. 18:15, 18).

Luke, in his Gospel, wrote that the Pharisees told Jesus to rebuke his followers for their shouts of praise (see Luke 19:39). No doubt they were afraid of what the Romans' reaction might be if it seemed the people were proclaiming Jesus king. John, in his Gospel, added a comment the Pharisees made to one another, no doubt in anger and frustration: "You see that you can do nothing; look, the world has gone after him" (John 12:19).

Jesus at the Temple (21:12-17)

All four Gospels include the incident of Jesus' cleansing of the Temple, though they vary in their timing of the event. According to Matthew, the Temple cleansing occurred on the same day as Jesus' entry into Jerusalem.

When he went into the Temple's Court of the Gentiles, Jesus found it busy with the activity of the money changers and sellers of sacrificial birds and animals. It was necessary for the pilgrims to be able to change their own currency into the coins required for the Temple tax. And, since sacrificial birds and animals had to be officially certified as unblemished, it was helpful to be able to purchase them there at the Temple itself. But evidently the selling and money changing had become a means of exploiting and cheating the people.

Jesus became angry at what he saw. He drove out the merchants and overturned the money changers' tables. He combined two references from the Old Testament to explain his action. In Isaiah 56:7, God had declared that his house would "be called a house of prayer for all peoples." In Jeremiah 7:11, God, through the prophet, had used the words "den of robbers" to describe what his house had become.

Jesus saw that the clamor of buying and selling, together with the cheating of the people, had made the Temple a place which could not fulfill its intent of being a place of prayer. In cleansing the Temple, Jesus had fulfilled the messianic prophecy found in Malachi 3:1,3; "the Lord whom you seek will suddenly come to his temple . . . and he will purify the sons of Levi and refine them like gold and silver, till they present right offerings to the Lord."

Children in the Temple continued the shout which had accompanied Jesus' entry into Jerusalem, "Hosanna to the Son of David!" (v. 15). They were proclaiming his messiahship.

Of course the chief priests and scribes "were indignant" (v. 15). Jesus was a threat to the scribes' authority and to the chief priests' prestige and source of profit.

The chief priests and scribes asked Jesus, "Do you hear what these are saying?" (v. 16). They considered the children's shouts a desecration of the Temple and blamed Jesus for them.

But Jesus used Psalm 8:2 to show these religious leaders how wrong they were (v. 16). The leaders might not acknowledge Jesus, but these children had.

Jesus then went outside Jerusalem to Bethany, where he spent the night. He may have stayed outside all night. Or he may have lodged with his friends Lazarus, Mary, and Martha who, according to John's Gospel, lived in Bethany.

The Fruitless Fig Tree (21:18-22)

On the following morning, as he traveled back to Jerusalem from Bethany, Jesus was hungry. He saw a fig tree in leaf by the side of the road and thought he would eat some figs from it. Upon closer inspection, however, he found that the tree had only leaves, no fruit.

Mark, in his account of this incident, wrote that "it was not the season for figs" (Mark 11:13). But sometimes small numbers of edible figs did appear early. The fruit actually started before the leaves. So the fact that the tree had leaves indicated that it should also have had at least the beginnings of some fruit.

Seeing that the tree was barren, Jesus declared that it would never again produce fruit. And the tree immediately withered. Why would Jesus have worked this destructive miracle? He was using the fig tree and its destruction to symbolize Israel and Israel's coming fate. To all outward appearances, Israel was full of the promise of spiritual fruit. Yet, in reality, Israel was fruitless. Like the fig tree, it would be destroyed because of its barrenness.

The withering of the fig tree amazed the disciples. They wondered how Jesus had brought the sudden miracle about. Jesus reminded them faith can always work miracles. Faith in God's ability can bring about the removal of even seemingly insurmountable difficulties (which he symbolized with the idea of a mountain being cast into the sea, v. 21).

Amazing resources are available through the prayer of faith (v. 22). Fruitlessness, then, does not have to be the fate of any individ-

ual or nation. Faith and faith's expression in prayer make it possible
to bear fruit for God.

A Question About Authority (21:23-27)

The question (21:23)—That same day, the day after the Temple
cleansing, Jesus went back and began teaching in the Temple. As he
taught, the chief priests and elders came to question him about his
authority. The chief priests were Sadducees. The elders were scribes
or Pharisees, the laymen. Together they made up the membership of
the Sanhedrin, the Jewish high council.

They felt they had the right to ask about the source of Jesus' authority. They had not given Jesus the authority to clear the Temple
of merchants and money changers. And they knew he had not even
been ordained as a rabbi. Yet he taught the people. If they had not
authorized him to do these things, who had?

Perhaps these authorities hoped Jesus would make an admission
which would enable them to take action against him. But Jesus knew
that it was not yet time for his earthly ministry to end. He was acting
on God's timetable, and much remained for him to do. So Jesus did
not want to verbally admit to being God's Son, the Messiah, at this
point.

Jesus' reply (21:24-25a).—Jesus agreed to answer the authorities'
question on the condition that they would first answer one for him.
He wanted them to tell him the source of authority for the baptism
of John the Baptist. Had it come from God or not? Since John had
claimed authority from God and had endorsed Jesus as sent from
God, the leaders' answer would relate to Jesus as well as to John.

The authorities' dilemma (21:25b-27).—Jesus' question created a
dilemma for the chief priests and elders. They realized that to admit
John's authority came from God would be to condemn themselves.
After all, John had preached an even more rigorous morality than
their own. Jesus would indict them for their lack of belief in John.
But if they claimed John's source of authority was a merely human
one, they would anger the people. The people believed that John
was a prophet, a messenger from God.

Neither answer seemed a safe one to make. The authorities decided then to claim ignorance. "We do not know" (v. 27), they told
Jesus, thereby evading the issue. Yet one of the jobs of the Sanhedrin

was to determine which prophets were true and which were false.

Since these leaders had not answered his question, Jesus insisted that he would not answer theirs. Since they were not able to judge John, they could not fairly judge Jesus either.

Jesus' Parable About Two Sons (21:28-32)

Jesus went on to tell the religious authorities a parable about two sons. Only Matthew has included this parable in his Gospel. In the story, a man told one of his two sons to work in his vineyard that day. The son refused his father's request. Later, however, the son was sorry that he had refused and did go and work.

The father also asked his second son to work in his vineyard. That son agreed to work but then did not do any work. Jesus asked the authorities to tell him which son had been obedient to the father. They correctly answered that the first one had been obedient.

Jesus declared that their own answer had condemned them. Sinners such as harlots and tax collectors would enter God's kingdom before they would. Like the second son, the authorities had promised they would do God's will. Yet they had not believed John, who had brought them God's demand for repentance.

At first the tax collectors and harlots had been far from God's kingdom. But they had believed John and had repented. In the end, they and not the self-righteous religious authorities had done God's will. God demands real obedience, not just lip service.

Jesus' Parable About a Vineyard's Tenants (21:33-46)

Jesus continued with yet another parable for the religious leaders. This one, told in allegorical form, was based in part upon Isaiah 5:1-7, a passage which would have been familiar to those who heard Jesus.

The story (21:33-39).—The story concerned a man "who planted a vineyard" (v. 33), equipping it with a hedge for protection from animals, a watch tower, and a winepress. Then he went abroad and left the vineyard in charge of tenants who agreed to pay their rent in the form of part of the yearly crop of fruit.

When the time came for the grapes to be ready, the owner sent some of his servants to get his share. Instead of giving the servants the fruit, however, the tenants savagely attacked them. One servant was beaten, one was stoned, and one was murdered. Still a second group of servants sent later by the owner received the same treatment.

Finally, the owner sent his own son to get the fruit, thinking that the tenants would surely respect him. But the servants did not respect the son. They killed him instead.

A question and an answer (21:40-41).—Jesus now turned and asked a question of the religious authorities. What, he asked, would the owner do to those tenants? They answered that the owner would naturally put them to death. Then he would give management of the vineyard to new tenants, who would give him the fruit he was due. As before, the authorities had condemned themselves with their own words.

The symbolism.—In the symbolism of the Old Testament, the vineyard stood for Israel. The owner in this parable was God himself. The tenants were the religious leaders of Israel. The servants were the prophets. And the son was, of course, Jesus. God had entrusted the nation of Israel to leaders who had not presented him with spiritual fruit. He had sent his prophets to warn them, but these had been killed instead of heeded. Amazingly, he had sent his own Son, in spite of the fate of his prophets. Soon the authorities would even have the Son killed. In so doing, they would be rebelling against God, trying to shut him out of the world he had made.

The corner stone (21:42-43).—Jesus quoted from Psalm 118:22-23 to warn the leaders about the consequences of rejecting him. That passage had spoken of a stone rejected by the builders but finally made "the head of the corner" (v. 42). That stone may be understood to be the cornerstone of a building or the crowning stone at the building's apex.

The Jewish authorities would reject Jesus; but God had chosen to make him head of a new "nation," (v. 43), a new people of God, who would produce the fruit he expected.

The kingdom would be taken from the leaders who had not been faithful to God's will. Keep in mind that God's people today also stand under his judgment when they fail to carry out the mission he had given them.

Invitations to a Wedding Feast (22:1-14)

Refusals (22:1-7).—Jesus then told the chief priests and elders a third parable. This story concerned a king who was planning a wedding feast for his son. In accordance with oriental custom, the king first sent out servants to give a general invitation to those the king had chosen to invite. Amazingly enough, those who were invited refused to accept the invitation.

Later, when the banquet was prepared, the king sent out still more servants to issue another invitation, giving the same people another chance. This time the message declared that everything was ready. But most of those who were invited made excuses for not going. And the rest did an incredible thing. They killed the servants who had brought them the invitation.

To refuse a king's invitation was to reject the authority of the king himself. To kill the king's servants as well was an offense requiring severe punishment for the murderers. The angry king sent out troops to destroy them and burn their city.

The banquet guests (22: 8-10).—But still the king was determined to fill the hall for his son's wedding feast. So he sent out servants to bring in all kinds of people, good and bad, from the streets. These, then, were the king's banquet guests.

Jesus was speaking here about the Jewish religious leaders. They thought they would be overjoyed to receive an invitation to God's banquet table. Yet they had been hostile or indifferent to the invitation when it had come through Jesus. For that reason, God had chosen to open the doors to his kingdom to all kinds of people. That was why Jesus' ministry extended to "sinners" and outcasts.

The guest without a wedding garment (22:11-14).—During the feast, the king, looking over the hall full of guests, saw one man who was not dressed for the occasion. The man was not wearing a wedding garment. It may have been customary for the host to furnish the wedding garments for the banquet guests. At the very least, the guests would have been expected to dress appropriately in clean, white clothing.

The man, when questioned, offered no excuse. So the king had him bound and thrown outside the lighted banquet hall into the darkness. There he could regret what he had done. Jesus closed this parable by saying that "many are called, but few are chosen" (v. 14).

What is the meaning of the incident of the man without the proper wedding clothes? This man was among the second group invited. He was like the tax collectors and harlots Jesus had invited into God's kingdom.

God wanted all these to receive his salvation. But moral demands went along with the gift of salvation. Those not clothed with repentance and righteousness would not be accepted.

God, in his grace, has called all people to receive his salvation. But those who accept God's salvation must accept it on his terms, living their lives according to his will.

Is It Right to Pay Taxes? (22:15-22)

Evidently these three parables enraged the religious authorities. For Matthew tells us the Pharisees then met to decide how best to trap Jesus.

They decided to send some of their own pupils along with some Herodians (who were in Jerusalem for Passover) to question Jesus. The alliance of the Pharisaic students and the Herodians was definitely a strange one. The Pharisees stood opposed to Roman rule, while the Herodians supported the rule of the Herods under the dominion of Rome. Only their mutual hatred of Jesus united them.

Together, these two groups came to Jesus. At first, they tried to disarm him with insincere flattery, calling him a true teacher of God's way and an impartial judge of people. Then they asked their question, a political one: "Is it lawful to pay taxes to Caesar, or not?" (v. 17).

They had chosen a highly controversial question. Whatever Jesus' answer might be, he would displease one of the groups. If he declared that payment of taxes to Caesar was lawful, he would infuriate the Pharisees. These would then spread the word of Jesus' opinion among the people and thereby turn them against him. But if he declared payment of taxes to Caesar to be unlawful, the Herodians could have him arrested for treason. The Pharisees and Herodians were sure they had Jesus in a trap from which he could not escape.

But Jesus knew they were trying to test him in order to destroy him. Calling them hypocrites, he asked for one of the coins with which the tax was to be paid. Then he asked his questioners to tell him whose image was on the coin. They answered that the image was Caesar's. This particular Caesar was Tiberius, who ruled from AD 14 to 37.

Jesus told them to give back to Caesar what belonged to Caesar. The emperor had the responsibility for the minting and circulating of the coins bearing his image. So the coins actually belonged to him. If he requested their return in the form of taxes, the people should give back what belonged to him.

But they must also give back to God what belongs to God. Each self bears God's image, and God wants each self given back to him in total allegiance.

Jesus' questioners marveled at his answer. They had no argument for it. For the time being, they left him.

The Sadducees' Question (22:23-33)

The questioners (22:23).—On that same day, some Sadducees came to question Jesus. The Sadducees were the small, wealthy aristocratic, priestly party. They based their religion on the first five books of the Old Testament. Unlike the Pharisees, they did not believe in resurrection from the dead, angels, or the oral tradition.

The question (22:24-28).—The Sadducees' question concerned the doctrine of resurrection. They used a deliberately exaggerated example, hoping, no doubt, to ensure that Jesus' answer would discredit him before the people. Their question was based on Moses' teaching in Deuteronomy 25:5-6.

Moses had taught that if brothers lived together, and one died childless, his brother should marry the widow in order to provide an heir for the dead brother. The Sadducees' question carried the possibilities of the law to an absurd extent. Suppose, they asked Jesus, seven brothers in turn married the woman, each dying without leaving a child. After her own death, whose wife would the woman be in the resurrection?

The Sadducees' point was that Moses must not have believed in the resurrection of the dead. Otherwise, he would have realized the consequences of carrying out this provision of the law. He would have seen how ridiculous it would be for a woman to have seven husbands in the resurrection.

Jesus' answer (22:29-32).—But Jesus declared that the Sadducees were doubly wrong. First, they assumed that any future life would have to be a continuation of this present, material life. They did not realize God's power to create a whole new order of things in the life to come. Marriage and the bearing of children are necessary on earth, where death is an ever-present fact. In the resurrection life, however, they will have no place.

Then Jesus told the Sadducees that their denial of the resurrection proved that they did not even understand their own Scriptures. He quoted from Exodus 3:6, part of the Scripture they accepted and claimed to understand.

In that verse God, speaking to Moses, had called himself "the God of Abraham, and the God of Isaac, and the God of Jacob" (v. 32). Yet those three men were already dead when God spoke. God, Jesus said, "is not the God of the dead, but of the living" (v. 32). He would not have described himself as the God of dead men.

The people's reaction (22:33).—The Sadducees had, no doubt, hoped to hurt Jesus' standing with the people by asking an unanswerable question. Instead, those in the crowd "were astonished at his teaching" (v. 33).

The Two Greatest Commandments (22:34-40)

The Pharisees may have been secretly pleased that Jesus "had silenced" (v. 34) their rivals, the Sadducees. Now, however, they gathered again to attempt to trap him.

One of the Pharisees, an expert in the law, asked Jesus what he considered to be the greatest of the law's commandments. The Pharisees recognized a total of 613 laws. Of them, 365 were negative commandments, while 248 were positive ones. Without hesitation, Jesus quoted Deuteronomy 6:5, a verse repeated daily by devout Jews. That verse demanded love for God with all one's being (v. 37).

But Jesus went on to give a similar and related commandment which was also of great importance. It came from Leviticus 19:18 and commanded that one love his neighbor as he loved himself. A person could not love God without also loving his neighbor. Neither could a person really love his neighbor unless he first loved God. To love one's neighbor as oneself would mean to want the same good for one's neighbor as for oneself. Jesus declared that all the law and prophets (the whole Old Testament) hung upon those two commandments.

If a person loves God with all his being, loves his fellow man, and also has a healthy respect for himself, he will keep all of God's commandments. No other commandments than the summary Jesus gave will be necessary.

Yet reducing the law to the commandment of love makes keeping God's law harder, not easier. For love demands far more than the mere keeping of written rules. Love requires total submission of one's life to God.

A Question for the Pharisees (22:41-46)

Now that the Pharisees and Sadducees had asked their questions, it was Jesus' turn to do some questioning of his own. Facing the gathered Pharisees, he asked for their opinion about "the Christ" (v. 42), meaning the Messiah. "Whose son is he?" (v. 42), Jesus asked.

The Jews generally held that the Messiah would be a son (descendant) of David. And in agreement with that belief, the Pharisees answered that the Messiah was to be David's son. You may remember that Matthew, in the very beginning of his Gospel, had affirmed that Jesus was "the son of David" (1:1). Usually, this title was interpreted as meaning a military leader who would reestablish Israel's earthly glory.

But Jesus reminded the Pharisees of a verse from Psalm 110, which was recognized by tradition as messianic in nature. In verse 1 of that psalm, David had called the Messiah his Lord. Moreover, he had referred to the Messiah as a transcendent being who would sit at God's right hand, not as a military conqueror.

Jesus asked the Pharisees how the Messiah could be David's son if David had called him his Lord. Jesus wanted the Pharisees to see that their concept of messiahship was simply too limited. They needed to see that the Messiah could be both transcendent, heavenly Lord and human descendant of David.

The Pharisees could not argue with Jesus' logical interpretation of the Scripture. Matthew wrote that no one dared asked him questions from that time on.

Criticism of the Scribes and Pharisees (23: 1-12)

Speaking to his disciples and to the gathered crowd, Jesus exposed
the faults of some of the scribes and Pharisees. But note as you read
that these tend to be the sins of religious people and leaders in every
age, including ours.

The scribes were experts in interpreting the Jewish law. Most of
them were Pharisees as well. The Pharisees were laymen (about six
thousand strong in Jesus' day) who devoted themselves to keeping
the scribal interpretations of the law. Jesus did not always disagree
with the teachings of the scribes and Pharisees. In fact, he held many
beliefs in common with them.

A warning (23:2-3).—Jesus told his audience to pay attention to
the teachings of these religious leaders. After all, they sat "on Moses'
seat" (v. 2), the chair in the synagogue from which the law's meaning was taught. But these leaders did not always practice what they
preached. So Jesus warned his hearers not to follow the example of
the scribes and Pharisees.

Faults of the leaders (23:4-10).—These religious authorities spe-
cialized in laying heavy burdens on the people by multiplying rules
and regulations about every phase of life. They did nothing to help
lighten the people's loads. They would "not move them with their
finger" (v. 4).

Several other characteristics of the scribes and Pharisees disturbed
Jesus. They loved, for instance, to show off their piety. They had to
have an audience for everything they did.

Jesus declared, for example, that they made "their phylacteries
broad and their fringes long" (v. 5). Phylacteries were leather cases
containing some verses from Exodus and Deuteronomy. They were
worn on the forehead and on the left arm. But Jesus charged that the
scribes and Pharisees made their phylacteries larger than was usual
so that they would seem more religious than other people. The
fringes were the tassels worn at the four corners of a garment to
remind the wearer of God's commandments. We know that Jesus
followed this custom (see 9:20). But the scribes and Pharisees were
lengthening their fringes to advertise their superior piety.

Jesus also saw the Pharisees and scribes always trying to get ahead
of everyone else. They wanted to sit at the right side of the host (the

place of honor) at feasts. They wanted to have the best seats in the synagogue. These seats may have been those which faced the congregation.

The religious leaders liked to be greeted with respect in the marketplace and to be called "rabbi" (v. 7). "Rabbi" was just then gaining use as a title for Jewish teachers. Jesus told his disciples not to be called "rabbi." They were all brothers with one teacher, Jesus himself.

Neither were Jesus' disciples to call any person "father" (v. 9), for they had God as their "one Father" (v. 9). Jesus was not speaking of a person's earthly, physical father in this instance. "Abba," or father, was used as a title for teachers and great leaders of the past. It may have sometimes been used as well for living people. Jesus saw that no one but God could give spiritual life and so deserve to be called a person's spiritual father. Jesus also told his disciples that they were not to be called "masters" (v. 10). He, "the Christ," was to be their "one master" (v. 10).

What makes a person great (23:11-12).—Once again Jesus repeated the principle he had often taught before. The truly great person is one who serves others. Those who exalt themselves at the expense of others will finally find themselves humbled. But God will exalt those who humble themselves in service to their fellow man and to him.

A Series of Accusations (23:13-36)

In a series of accusations, each preceded by "Woe to you," Jesus continued to criticize the hypocrisy he saw in the lives of the scribes and Pharisees. These "woes" were expressions of grief and sorrow uttered out of concern for the wrongs these religious leaders were doing to other people and for the punishment they were about to bring to themselves.

Shutting people out of the kingdom (23:13).—Jesus first accused the scribes and Pharisees of shutting people out of God's kingdom. They had taught that acceptance by God came only by the keeping of all the law, including the scribal interpretations of it. Many found such observances impossible. These leaders refused to accept Jesus' invitation to enter the kingdom by faith and repentance. And they kept others from doing so as well. The Revised

Standard Version does not include verse 14 as part of the original text of Matthew.

The problem of their proselytes (23:15).—In Jesus' day, Judaism did have a missionary effort. Jesus said that the scribes and Pharisees would "traverse sea and land to make a single proselyte" (v. 15). But then they would weigh that proselyte down under their law, making him twice as Pharisaic, ("twice as much a child of hell" v. 15), as they themselves were.

Insincere oaths (23:16-22).—Jesus had mentioned the subject of oaths in his Sermon on the Mount (see 5:33-37). There he had made it clear that no oaths are necessary for an honest person.

But the scribes and Pharisees had, in a sense, made perjury legal with their teachings on oaths. For instance, if a person swore by the Temple, he did not have to keep his oath. He did have to keep his oath if he swore by the gold on the Temple. Jesus recognized that no matter what a person might swear by, whether the Temple, the altar, or heaven, all belonged to God. The person who swore by them was calling God as a witness to his promise and was bound by it.

Tithing the little; neglecting the great (23:23-24).—The scribes had gone beyond the written law and decreed that a person must even make a tithe of the garden herbs such as "mint and dill and cummin" (v. 23). Jesus said that the Pharisees and scribes had meticulously tithed these tiny herbs. But they had meanwhile neglected the really important aspects of the law. Jesus put his emphasis on "justice and mercy and faith" (v. 23) as the law's major demands. He used a startling but memorable exaggeration, saying that these religious leaders strained what they drank to avoid swallowing a gnat but then swallowed a camel.

Only clean on the outside (23:25-26).—Jesus compared the scribes and Pharisees to cups and plates which are clean on the outside but dirty on the inside. These men tried hard through their rituals to keep the appearance of being very religious. But their religion did not always extend to their inner lives. If they had first been right with God (clean) on the inside, that purity would then have expressed itself in right outward actions.

Like whitewashed tombs (23:27-28).—Before Passover, tombs were whitewashed so that pilgrims could see them easily and not be defiled by walking on them. Of course the whitewashing beautified them too. Jesus saw that the scribes and Pharisees were like those whitewashed tombs. On the outside all appeared to be well. Inside, however, they were full of decay.

Completing the work of their fathers (23:29-36).—The ancestors of the scribes and Pharisees had killed the prophets God had sent to them. Jesus observed that the religious leaders had built tombs for the prophets their ancestors had killed. And they had sworn that they would not have behaved as their fathers had.

But they were about to complete their fathers' work by killing Jesus and others who would come in his name. Jesus declared that punishment would come to that generation for its deeds. Here he was likely speaking of the coming destruction of Jerusalem.

A Lament for Jerusalem (23:37-39)

Knowledge of Jerusalem's approaching destruction filled Jesus with the deepest sorrow. Lovingly, he lamented the choices this city had made. Jerusalem had decisively rejected every overture God had made toward her. Instead of listening to the prophets, Jerusalem had stoned them.

Jesus spoke of "how often" (v. 37) he would have gathered the children of Jerusalem as a mother hen (or bird) gathers her chicks "under her wing" (v. 37). Two verses from the Psalms are reflected in Jesus' thought here about the shelter he longed to give to Jerusalem's people (see Pss. 17:8 and 57:1). The phrase "how often" (v. 37) reminds us that the Synoptic Gospels (Matthew, Mark, and Luke) have left out a great deal about Jesus' work in Judea. John's Gospel includes much more about this phase of his ministry. Evidently Jesus had made appeal after appeal to Jerusalem's people on many occasions.

Jesus knew that Jerusalem could have escaped her coming fate if only she had accepted him and his way. Because she had rejected him and what he stood for, she would be destroyed only forty years later by the Roman armies. Because Jerusalem had rejected God's Son, God would withdraw his presence from the city and its Temple, leaving them "forsaken and desolate" (v. 38).

Like the prophets before him, Jesus would soon face death. But, he assured his hearers, his death would not be the end. He would come again in glory at the end of the age. And at that coming all would echo the acclamation of the crowds at Jesus' royal entry into Jerusalem, "Blessed is he who comes in the name of the Lord" (v. 39).

Teachings About Jerusalem's Destruction and the End of the Age
24:1 to 25:46

A Prediction and Three Questions (24:1-3)

As Jesus and his disciples were leaving the Temple, the disciples remarked to him about the Temple buildings. These must have been a beautiful and awe-inspiring sight. This Temple, the third which had stood on Mount Moriah, covered thirteen acres. Herod the Great had begun building it in 19 BC.

The magnificent white marble Temple complex must have appeared indestructible. But Jesus told his disciples that the day was coming when the Temple would be totally destroyed. The gigantic stones of which the buildings were composed would be leveled.

Later, as Jesus was sitting "on the Mount of Olives" (v. 3), his disciples came to question him about his prediction. No doubt they had been greatly disturbed to hear that the Temple would be destroyed. To them such a catastrophic happening had to be connected to the end of the age, the time when Jesus would return. So they asked Jesus to tell them when this destruction would take place and what the sign of his coming and of the age's end would be.

A Warning Not to Misread Events (24:4-14)

Jesus began his answer by speaking to the question about the sign of the end of the age. He warned his disciples not to allow themselves to be led astray. There would be many false Messiahs. His disciples should be sure not to follow any of these.

In history and in nature, there would be catastrophic events. Wars, famines, and earthquakes would occur, as they have occurred throughout the centuries. Jesus warned his disciples against believing that the occurrence of these events meant that the end had come. Such events were only the beginning of the birthpangs of the age which would come with the end of this present age.

The time between Jesus' earthly life and earth's end time would be marked also by sufferings in the church. Persecutions and executions of Christians would occur. Partly because of these, many within the church would lose faith and love and be misled by false prophets. But those who endured "to the end" (v. 13) would be saved (here meaning vindicated at the final judgment). The proof of a person's salvation would be his faithful endurance to the end.

In spite of the difficulties in the world and in the church, the gospel, the good news of God's rule through Christ, would "be preached throughout the whole world, as a testimony to all nations" (v. 14). Only after the completion of that worldwide mission would the end take place.

About Jerusalem's Coming Destruction (24:15-28)

Then Jesus began to explain about the coming destruction of Jerusalem. He spoke of the sight of "the desolating sacrilege" (v. 15) as the sign that it was time to flee the city. Daniel had spoken of an "abomination that makes desolate" (Dan. 12:11). That reference was to a Syrian ruler's (Antiochus Epiphanes') placing of a heathen altar on the Temple's altar of burnt offering in 168 BC.

A look at this passage's parallel in Luke's Gospel shows that the sight about which Jesus spoke was the appearance of Roman soldiers surrounding Jerusalem (see Luke 21:20). Jerusalem would then no longer be a safe place to stay.

Jesus advised that any of his disciples who were in Judea at that time should "flee to the mountains" (v. 16). (When the crisis did come in AD 70, they fled to Pella, one of the cities of the Decapolis.) This crisis would be so sudden and so full of peril that no one should even pause to collect any of his belongings.

Pregnant women and those with babies would have a hard time escaping from the city. If the crisis came in winter, travel would be difficult. And those with strong convictions against sabbath travel should pray that the crisis not come on a sabbath.

Escape would be all-important. For Jerusalem's destruction would be associated with unbelievably great tribulation. In fact, Jesus declared, if God had not chosen to shorten those days, none of his people would have been spared.

The siege of Jerusalem would bring with it claims that a messianic deliverance from Rome was about to occur. Some would say that the Messiah was in the wilderness, preparing to lead an army of followers against Rome. Others would report that the Messiah was in some secret place. Jesus warned his disciples not to believe any of these false messianic claims, even if they were accompanied by miracles.

Jesus' return as the Messiah, the Son of man, would not be an event known only to a few. Instead, it would be visible to all people at once, like lightning which flashes across the sky. This coming in judgment would take place just as surely as vultures gather where a body is present (v. 28).

Signs of the Coming of the Son of Man (24:29-31)

Jesus had warned his disciples against believing that wars, earthquakes, and famines were signs of the end (see vv. 6-3). But he went on to tell them the signs which would announce his coming at the end of the age.

These signs would involve spectacular disruptions of the natural order. Sun and moon would no longer give light. The stars would fall from their height. The very "powers of the heavens" would "be shaken" (v. 29). These events would mark history's end. Then "the sign of the Son of man" (v. 30) would appear. This sign might well be the appearance of Jesus himself. At the sight of him, all of earth's people would mourn their part in his death or their failure to recognize him (see Zech. 12:10-14).

Jesus' first coming to earth had been in the form of Suffering Servant. But all the people would see him in his second coming as the heavenly Son of man prophesied in the book of Daniel (see Dan. 7:13-14). He would be seen coming on heaven's clouds with glory and power. His angels would then gather together those who were his own.

The Fig Tree's Lesson (24:32-35)

Jesus used the fig tree as an illustration of a sign pointing to a coming event. He reminded his disciples that the appearance of leaves on a fig tree means "that summer is near" (v. 32). In a similar way, he told them, the occurrence of "all these things," would mean that "he is near, at the very gates" (v. 33).

Verses 32-35 pose a difficult problem in interpretation. To what, for example, do "all these things" (v. 33) refer? Was Jesus speaking of the events which would precede Jerusalem's destruction? Or was he referring to the signs which would precede and accompany his coming at the end of the age?

"He is near" (v. 33) can just as easily be translated "it is near" (KJV), since there is no subject expressed in the Greek text of this verse. If "it" is the intended translation, likely Jesus was speaking of the destruction of Jerusalem. This likelihood seems even more probable when we consider that Jesus declared "this generation" would "not pass away till all these things take place" (v. 34). His generation had not yet passed away when Jerusalem was destroyed in AD 70.

Jesus went on to promise the disciples that his words had eternal significance. Earth and heaven will not last forever in their present forms. But Jesus' words will always endure (v. 35). Both Jerusalem's destruction and Jesus' return were sure to occur because he had declared that they would.

Watch and Be Ready (24:36-44)

Jesus told his disciples that the exact hour and day of his second coming were known only to God the Father. Even he, God's Son, did not share in the knowledge of the time of the end. The fact that God alone has this knowledge should warn us not to waste time trying to predict when the end will come.

Jesus did say that the time of his coming would be similar to the time of the flood in Noah's day. Back then people were carrying on all the normal activities of life— "eating and drinking, marrying and giving in marriage" (v. 38). Of course there is nothing wrong with these things. But the people in Noah's time were so absorbed in them that they were totally unprepared when the flood came. Only Noah and his family had made preparation. It was too late for the others.

Jesus explained that at the time of his return, a separation would take place. Two men, for instance, might be working together in a field. One would be taken while the other would be left. One woman "grinding at the mill" (v. 41) would be taken, while the one beside her would be left. The criterion for judgment would be the individual's state of readiness for Jesus' return.

Jesus then used the example of a homeowner whose house had been robbed. There is a possibility that he was talking about an actual recent incident known to his hearers. The homeowner probably lived in an ordinary house with walls made of baked clay. The thief may have dug through a wall to enter the house.

Jesus told the disciples that the man had been unable to prevent the thief from entering the house because he did not know when the thief was coming. The thief certainly didn't announce his intentions in advance. So the man lost his possessions through lack of watchfulness.

Jesus' advice, then, was that his followers watch and be ready for his return. They should not become so absorbed in worldly things that they would forget eternal things. The fact of his coming is a certainty. But it will come as suddenly and as unexpectedly as the flood came in Noah's day or as a thief comes in any day.

A Challenge to Faithfulness (24:45-51)

Because Jesus would soon be physically leaving his disciples, he wanted to instruct them in how to live for him in his absence. They would have to do more than watch for his return. They would also need to be faithful in the work they had to do. For teaching, Jesus used the example of a servant appointed to be manager of his master's household while the master was away.

A "faithful and wise servant" (v. 45) would be one dedicated to the job he had been given and capable of using good judgment. He would take care of the needs of the household servants. The master, on his return, would find that servant busy at his assigned duties. And in appreciation, he would promote that servant to a position of even greater responsibility.

But if a "wicked servant" (v. 48) had been given the same job of household manager, the results would be very different. That servant would decide he didn't need to work hard, since his master might not return for a long time. He would abuse the other servants and take advantage of his master's absence to do whatever he pleased. The master, returning unexpectedly, would be angry at that servant for failing to do the job with which he had been entrusted. He would punish that servant severely.

Jesus' message here was especially for his disciples who would have charge of directly ministering to other Christians. But it applies as well to all Christians in their doing of the work Christ has given them.

Jesus' point was that his followers needed to be faithful in their duty all the time. They could not assume that Jesus' return would be far in the future. That coming could be at any time. They needed to live and work always as if his coming were at hand.

Judgment would rest on "the hypocrites" (v. 51), those who claimed to be faithful servants when they really were not. These could expect no better fate than the scribes and Pharisees Jesus had so often condemned for their hypocrisy.

The Wise and the Foolish (25:1-13)

Jesus used a parable about a wedding to stress the need for preparation for his return. The main characters in this parable were ten maidens waiting for the arrival of the bridegroom. All ten carried lamps, since the festivities were taking place at night.

But the bridegroom did not come when expected. Because of the delay, the maidens slept. At midnight, however, they were awakened by the news that the bridegroom was finally coming.

Little oil was left in the maidens' lamps after the long wait. This was no problem for five of the maidens who had wisely brought flasks of oil. But the other five had foolishly not prepared for a possible delay. They had no extra oil.

The five who had extra oil had only enough for themselves. They told the others to go and buy more. Though it was midnight, it is possible that all the villagers were out for the wedding celebration and some merchant might have been willing to sell them oil.

By the time these five maidens returned from buying oil, the bridegroom had already come. He and his procession had gone in to the marriage feast, and the door was closed. The bridegroom refused to let the latecomers in.

Jesus' advice was that his followers watch, since they could not know the time of his return. This parable makes it clear that Jesus' return might be delayed. His followers, then, are to prepare for the possibility of that delay. They are always to be prepared for his coming, or for death, by living for God in the here and now. At some point there will no longer be time to prepare. The parable emphasizes also the fact that no one can make spiritual preparation for another person. Each person is responsible for his own faithfulness to God.

The Parable of the Talents (25:14-30)

Jesus told another parable to emphasize the importance of responsibly using one's God-given gifts in the time before Christ's return. He spoke of a man who was getting ready for a journey. Before he left, the man turned his monetary assets over to three of his servants for management in his absence. The assets were given in the form of "talents," a measure of weight of money in silver or gold. Today we call a person's abilities "talents" because of this parable.

This master gave his most capable servant five talents to manage. The second most capable received two talents. And the third received one talent. The five-talent servant used his money so well that he doubled it. The two-talent servant did the same. But the one-talent servant, fearful of losing the money, hid it in a hole in the ground.

When the master returned after a long absence, he called the three servants in for an accounting. He had only praise for the first two servants. They had handled his assets so capably that he would reward them with even greater responsibility.

The third servant tried to excuse his failure to productively use his master's money. He explained that his fear of investing the money had come from knowledge that the master was "a hard man" (v. 24).

The master had nothing but condemnation for this servant. He declared that at the very least the servant could have invested the money for interest. And so he ordered the one talent given to the one who could make the best use of it—the servant who already had ten talents.

The servants' master commented that those who make use of what they have will receive even more. Those who fail to use what they have will even lose that. The third servant was punished. And there will also be judgment for those who fail to use the gifts with which God has entrusted them.

In this parable Jesus taught that each individual is responsible for the use of only those gifts and abilities God has given him or her. Some people have more of these than others. There should be no comparing of capabilities for service to God, only the best use of one's own gifts, whether many or few.

A Parable About the Final Judgment (25:31-46)

In Matthew 16:27, Jesus had stated that "the Son of man is to come with his angels in the glory of his Father, and then he will repay every man for what he has done." Jesus' last parable in Matthew's Gospel (25:31-46) tells us how (on what basis) that repayment will be made. You will notice that this parable differs from the others. It is a vivid, poetic word picture foretelling the way Jesus will judge the world.

The parable pictures Jesus as the heavenly Son of man, seated on a throne, surrounded by angels. In the parable, Jesus is described as judge, King, and shepherd. As the people of all nations stand before him, Jesus will make a separation. He will act as a shepherd acts in separating the goats from the sheep. (Since goats were black and sheep white, such separating was easy for the shepherd.) In this parable "sheep" symbolize God's righteous people. "Goats" symbolize the unrighteous.

At the last judgment, Jesus will put the "sheep" at his right hand, the place of favor. The "goats" will be at his left. He will invite the "sheep" to share in his Father's kingdom because of their ministry to him on earth. He will declare that they had fed him, quenched his thirst, welcomed him when he was a stranger, clothed him when he was naked, visited him when he was sick and when he was in prison.

The righteous will be totally surprised. When, they will ask, had they ever done these things for Jesus? And Jesus will tell them that in performing these acts of kindness for those in need, they performed them for him. That is how total Jesus' identification with suffering humanity is.

This Jesus will turn to the "goats" on his left. For them the verdict is a different one, though the criterion for judgment is the same. These are to face "the eternal fire" (v. 41) because they did not care for Jesus when he was suffering. These too will question Jesus. They cannot remember ever seeing Jesus sick, naked, thirsty, hungry, or imprisoned. If they had, they would surely have ministered to him.

And Jesus will solemnly tell them that he was present in all the suffering people they did encounter. By not ministering to these, they were failing to minister to him. "Eternal punishment" (v. 46) is the fate which awaits these. But "eternal life" (v. 46) is the reward of the righteous.

The main point of this parable seems at first glance to run counter to the teaching that belief in Jesus is sufficient to enable a person to receive eternal life. But mere profession of belief which does not lead to active love and concern for others is useless and insincere. Those who received punishment were those who let their concern for themselves blot out compassion for others.

We cannot be sure of the exact meaning behind "eternal fire" and "eternal punishment." But we can be sure that they are the complete opposite of the eternal life God wants to give to those who will receive it.

Ever-Darkening Events
26:1-56

A Prediction and a Plot (26:1-5)

The prediction (26:1-2).—At the end of Jesus' teaching there on the Mount of Olives (see 24:3 to 25:46), Jesus predicted for the fourth time (according to Matthew's record) that he would soon die. This time he added something new to his prediction. His death by crucifixion would take place during Passover, which would begin in two days. Passover annually commemorated the Jews' deliverance from slavery in Egypt.

The plot (26:3-5).—Meanwhile, the elders and chief priests, members of the Sanhedrin (the Jewish high court), were plotting Jesus' death. They met at the palace of Caiaphas, who was then the high priest. (He kept this office from AD 18 to 36.)

These religious leaders were agreed on the necessity of putting Jesus to death, but the timing was a problem for them. They feared that to arrest Jesus openly during Passover might lead to an uprising of the people. The Sadducees especially owed their offices and power to the continuing goodwill of Rome. And Rome would not tolerate any rebellion among the Jews.

Jesus' arrest, then, would have to be made "by stealth" (v. 4). And it was agreed that he should not be arrested and executed during Passover—when nationalistic feelings were running high, and many of Jesus' followers from Galilee were gathered in Jerusalem. Soon, however, an unexpected happening changed the authorities' assessment of the situation (see vv. 14-16).

An Anointing at Bethany (26:6-13)

At Bethany one day, Jesus was at the home of a man called Simon the leper. No doubt Simon had formerly been a leper but had been cured, perhaps by Jesus.

During the meal at Simon's house a woman, unnamed by Matthew (but identified in John 12:3 as Mary of Bethany), did an unusual thing. She took the possession which was probably her most valuable, an alabaster flask of ointment, and poured its contents on Jesus' head.

What was the woman's motive? Matthew did not mention one. Some have suggested that she was anointing Jesus as king. Certainly messianic symbolism was present in her action, whether she realized it or not. But more likely, she had heard about the threats of Jesus' enemies and realized the end would come soon for him. She wanted to show her love for him in this sacrificial way while there was still time.

For Jesus, this woman's generous act must have been like a ray of sunshine in an otherwise dark time. But his disciples failed to understand. In fact "they were indiganant" (v. 8) at what they saw as sheer waste. They protested that the ointment should have been sold and the proceeds given to the poor.

According to Mark 14:5, the disciples estimated the ointment's value at "more than three hundred denarii." This amount represented nearly a year's wages for a laborer.

A short while before, Jesus had spoken of the importance of helping all those in need (25:31-46). He had even made this love in action the criterion for judgment. But now he defended the woman to the disciples. He appreciated her great love which had caused her to give sacrificially without counting the cost.

Jesus reminded the disciples that there would always be poor people to help. He was not using that fact to excuse failure to help the poor. He was simply trying to help the disciples see that the time for showing love for him was limited; the time for helping the poor was not.

The same kind of ointment could be used both for anointing kings and in burying the dead. While the anointing could be seen as a symbolic anointing of Jesus as king, Jesus saw that the woman had actually been anointing his body for burial. He *would be* the messianic king, but he would also be a crucified king. The woman's sacrifice was a symbol of the much greater sacrifice he would soon make for all people.

Jesus declared that the fragrance of the woman's loving sacrifice would linger on. The story of her anointing of Jesus would be told wherever his gospel was preached. At this critical time in his life, what a contrast Jesus must have seen between the openly loving and generous act of the woman and the petty, critical attitude of his disciples.

Judas' Offer of Betrayal (26:14-16)

The religious authorities had been looking for an opportunity to arrest Jesus without creating a disturbance among the people. Their objective became unexpectedly easier when Judas, "one of the twelve" (v. 14), came to the chief priests with an offer to betray Jesus.

The chief priests agreed to pay Judas the amount of thirty shekels, the price of a slave. In exchange, Judas would "deliver" (v. 15) Jesus to them. It seems that Judas agreed to help the authorities find and arrest Jesus at a time when the crowds would not be able to protest. Judas knew where Jesus spent his nights, and so he could guide those who would be making the arrest.

Matthew wrote that Judas, from then on, looked for a chance to betray Jesus. The question we have to ask is: Why did Judas betray Jesus? There are several possibilities.

Judas may have simply been greedy for the money he could be paid for betrayal. John, in his account of the supper at Bethany, included the information that Judas was a thief who stole from the disciples' money box. Yet the amount of money involved here seems too small to account for such a treacherous act. Greed may have played a part in Judas' betrayal of Jesus but was probably not his major motive.

It seems likely that Judas had decided Jesus was the great leader who would free the Jews from Rome. Judas may, in fact, have been a Zealot, one who advocated revolt against the Romans. It is possible that when Judas finally saw that Jesus would not be a political Messiah, he decided to betray him, out of anger and disillusionment. His earlier feelings of hope and trust in Jesus may, in the end, have turned to hatred.

A third possibility is that Judas betrayed Jesus in order to force Jesus to proclaim himself a political Messiah. Judas may have believed that if he had Jesus arrested, Jesus would feel compelled to start a revolt against Rome.

The Gospels themselves do not tell us Judas' motive. Luke and John do tell us that "Satan entered into Judas" (Luke 22:3; see also John 13:27).

Whatever Judas' motive in betraying Jesus may have been, it is clear that he was not willing to accept Jesus for what he was. He had decided what Jesus should be and wanted to make Jesus fit that image. Judas had been one of Jesus' twelve close disciples. He should have known Jesus as well as anyone did. Yet he betrayed him. That fact should warn Christians even today that they too might seek to make Jesus over in their image. To change Jesus to fit into personal schemes is to betray him.

Preparations for the Passover Meal (26:17-19)

Matthew wrote that "on the first day of Unleavened Bread" (v. 17) the disciples asked Jesus for instructions about where they should prepare the Passover meal. This meal had to be eaten within the city of Jerusalem. Since space was at a premium, those who had traveled to Jerusalem for the feast had to borrow rooms from residents for celebrating Passover.

Evidently Jesus had already made arrangements for a room at the home of one of his Jerusalem followers. He instructed the disciples to find a certain man in the city and give him Jesus' message. The message was that Jesus' time had now come. He and his disciples would eat their Passover meal at this man's house.

The disciples followed Jesus' instructions and prepared the meal. The lamb for the meal (if this were a complete Passover dinner) had to be slaughtered that afternoon in the Temple. The meal would begin after six o'clock that evening.

A Foretelling of Betrayal (26:20-25)

That night Jesus and his disciples shared the Passover meal together. They probably reclined on couches to eat, rather than sitting down. As they ate, Jesus solemnly told his disciples that one of them would betray him. Judas had kept his plans secret from the other disciples, but Jesus knew what was in Judas' heart.

This news upset the disciples greatly. "One after another," they asked Jesus, "Is it I, Lord?" (v. 22). Except for Judas, each of the disciples was sure of his love for Jesus. Yet how could any of them be confident of remaining loyal if testing became severe?

Jesus did not give them a definite identification of his betrayer. He did say that one who had dipped food into the dish with him would betray him. No doubt several of them had done this at one time. Psalm 41:9, which speaks of the treachery of a friend with whom one had eaten, must have been in Jesus' mind.

Jesus went on to say that he would fulfill the role of which the prophets had written. He would be the Suffering Servant and the shepherd dying for his sheep (see Isa. 53:3-8 and Zech. 13:7). But though he was fulfilling his ordained role, he lamented the fate of his betrayer, saying it would have been better if that man had not been born. It is possible that Jesus was giving Judas one last opportunity to repent.

According to Matthew, it was only at this point that Judas asked, "Is it I, Master?" (v. 25). The others may not have heard Jesus' answer, "You have said so" (v. 25). Very likely, Jesus meant "Yes."

The Bread and the Cup (26:26-29)

During the meal, Jesus took, blessed, and broke bread. As he gave it to his disciples, he told them to eat the bread. It represented his body. Soon that body would be given for them in death.

After Jesus had said a prayer of thanksgiving, he gave the cup to his disciples, telling them all to drink from it. The cup represented Jesus' "blood of the covenant" (v. 28) which would soon be "poured out for many for the forgiveness of sins" (v. 28).

In Exodus 24:6-8, Moses had thrown the blood of oxen on the altar and on the people to seal the covenant between God and the people. Jesus was now establishing a new covenant by his death. This new covenant would fulfill Jeremiah 31:31-34. It would not be a covenant based on law but would instead be based on faith and repentance. God would enter into this new relationship with his people through the shedding of Jesus' blood. His blood represented the life Jesus would give for others. His death for others would fulfill Isaiah 53:11 which had declared that God's righteous servant would "make many to be accounted righteous."

Jesus saw this meal as a foretaste of the one he would someday share with his followers in the kingdom of his Father. It was believed that the messianic banquet would inaugurate the new age. Not until the time of that banquet would Jesus again share the cup with his disciples. This Supper, meanwhile, was a pledge of the certainty of the kingdom's establishment and their sharing together in it.

The Passover meal was a remembrance of God's freeing of the Israelites from slavery in Egypt. The blood of a lamb, smeared on the lintel and doorposts of the Israelites' houses, had saved their children from death (see Ex. 12:21-27). Jesus was now establishing a new Passover which would commemorate the freeing of people from slavery to sin. He was the new Passover sacrifice.

A Prediction of Denial (26:30-35)

After they had finished the Passover meal, Jesus and the disciples sang a hymn, probably taken from Psalms 115—118. Then "they went out to the Mount of Olives" (v. 30).

Jesus then told his disciples that he would be the cause of their stumbling, or falling away, that night. He quoted Zechariah 13:7. He was the shepherd. The disciples were his little flock which would be scattered because of his coming arrest and execution.

But there was a note of hope. Jesus repeated that he would be raised. Death would not be the end for him. And after his resurrection, he would precede the disciples to Galilee. In spite of the weakness they would soon demonstrate, he looked forward to being with them again.

It seems that Peter had heard only the prediction that all the disciples would fail Jesus. Jesus' words about his resurrection must have fallen on deaf ears. Peter was sure of himself and his loyalty to Jesus. He declared that all the others might "fall away" (v. 33) because of Jesus, but he never would.

But Jesus knew Peter far better than Peter knew himself. He told Peter that that very night "before the cock crows" (v. 34), Peter would deny him three times. "Cock crow" was the name given to the third Roman watch of the night (12:00 AM to 3:00 AM). In this case, however, it seems that Jesus was speaking of daybreak, with the literal crowing of a rooster.

Peter could not accept Jesus' prediction. He assured Jesus that he would never deny him, even if he had to die with him. All the other disciples then voiced confidence in their own loyalty as well (though, according to John 13:30, Judas had left them during the Last Supper).

Peter probably would have willingly fought and died for Jesus that night if Jesus had declared himself a military Messiah and ordered a revolt against Rome. But Peter would find himself unequal to testing when it came in an unexpected form.

A Time of Agonizing Prayer (26:36-46)

The scene at Gethsemane (26:36-38).—Jesus then went with his disciples to Gethsemane (the name meant "oil press"). This was probably a garden on the Mount of Olives. There Jesus wanted to pray. He instructed eight of the disciples to stay outside. But he took with him the three who were closest to him—Peter, James, and John.

Jesus told these three about the anguish he was experiencing. He described his sorrow as being as great as death's sorrow. He wanted these disciples to give him human sympathy and support to help him through his ordeal. He asked them to watch with him.

Jesus' prayers and the disciples' weakness (26:39-44).—Going a short distance from the three, Jesus fell prostrate on the ground. His prayer, in summary, was for his Father to somehow save him from having to endure the death ("cup," v. 39) he was about to face. Yet, he concluded his prayer with a declaration of his willingness to do his Father's will.

Jesus then went back to the three disciples and found they had fallen asleep. They had not been able to stay awake even an hour with him. Their lack of sympathy and understanding must have increased the sadness he was feeling at that moment. He told them to "watch and pray" (v. 41) that they might have strength for facing temptation (testing). He knew that they were spiritually willing, but their human weaknesses could easily cause them to stumble.

Again, for a time, Jesus prayed for God's will to be done. And again he found the disciples asleep. Yet a third time he prayed the prayer, and still the disciples slept.

The meaning of this time of prayer (26:45-46).—But the time for sleeping was now past. Jesus' "hour" (v. 45) had come. In a sense, victory was already his. There in the garden he had come through the severest testing of his earthly life. Never had the temptation to save himself been stronger. But Jesus had submitted himself to the will of his Father and so would be able to save others.

Why was Jesus so anguished as he prayed in Gethsemane? We can never know the depths of his experience there. But the fact that he would be the bearer of the world's sin may help explain his agony. He was facing as well rejection by the people he had come to save and a lack of understanding sympathy even from his own disciples.

No other recorded experience of Jesus reveals his human side so vividly. It is only because he endured such human agony and testing that he can strengthen us in our times of sorrow and temptation and sympathize with us.

Jesus realized that his enemies were on their way to arrest him. Instead of running away, he chose to face them. Only by so doing could he complete his mission of salvation.

Arrest in the Garden (26:47-56)

Judas arrived at the garden with an armed crowd ready to arrest Jesus. The crowd was evidently made up of the Temple guard and servants of the high priest. Those who had come to make the arrest did not know Jesus. So Judas had agreed to identify Jesus with a sign. He would kiss Jesus, as was customary for a disciple greeting his master.

Even in the face of Judas' treachery, Jesus reacted with sadness instead of anger. He called Judas "Friend" (v. 50), still holding the door of repentance open for him.

Jesus had no intention of resisting arrest. But one of his disciples, identified by John as Peter, responded to Jesus' arrest with violence. With his sword, he cut off the ear of a slave of the high priest. Jesus would not allow the violence to continue, because he knew it was not the answer for him or for his nation. According to Luke's account of this incident, Jesus healed the slave's ear (see Luke 22:51).

Jesus reminded all those present that even then he had only to ask and his Father would send "more than twelve legions of angels" (v. 53) to rescue him. But Scripture required that he endure arrest and death.

Jesus thought it strange that this armed band had come out to arrest him at night, as if he were a dangerous criminal. They could easily have arrested him on any of the days he had openly taught in the Temple. But then they would have had to answer to the crowds who followed him. Jesus saw the manner of his arrest as fulfilling the words of the prophets. He must have especially seen fulfillment of Isaiah's description of God's Servant as one who "was numbered with the transgressors" (Isa. 53:12).

It seems that the orders were to arrest only Jesus, not his followers. Perhaps the authorities felt that the death of the leader would put an end to all he had begun. Confronted with Jesus' failure to resist and refusal to let them fight for him, the disciples all fled. Jesus would have to face his ordeal alone.

Triumph Out of Seeming Defeat
26:57 to 28:20

At Caiaphas' Palace (26:57-68)

Matthew next described a hearing which took place at the palace of the high priest, Caiaphas. According to John, there had been a brief earlier hearing before Annas, the former high priest, the father-in-law of Caiaphas (see John 18:13).

Peter had fled with the rest of the disciples when Jesus was arrested. He had returned, however, to see what was happening. In the high priest's courtyard, Peter "sat with the guards to see the end" (v. 58).

Inside the palace, the Sanhedrin was meeting, though the council was not supposed to meet at night. It seems that this meeting was an informal hearing rather than an actual trial. These religious leaders were anxious to find some charge against Jesus worthy of the death penalty. False witness after false witness appeared to give testimony. But no two had the agreeing testimony required by the law.

Finally, two witnesses testified that Jesus had claimed to be able to destroy God's Temple and rebuild it in three days' time. To speak against the Temple was considered blasphemy. This testimony was a total distortion of Jesus' words. He had actually claimed that if the temple of his body were destroyed, he would raise it in three days (see John 2:19-21). Jesus refused to answer the charge, knowing it would be useless to try to defend himself. After all, the minds of the members of the Sanhedrin were already made up.

The high priest then put Jesus under oath. He demanded that Jesus tell the council whether he was "the Christ, the Son of God" (v. 63). If Jesus' answer were affirmative, he could be accused of being a revolutionary. Jesus' answer, "You have said so" (v. 64), implied that he *was* God's Son, the Messiah. But he went on to interpret those titles. He was no political Messiah. Instead, he was the heavenly Son of man who would fulfill the words of Psalm 110:1 and Daniel 7:13.

To the high priest, however, Jesus' words were blasphemy. A person was supposed to tear his clothing upon hearing a blasphemy. This the high priest did. He declared that there was no more need for witnesses, since Jesus was obviously guilty of blasphemy. And the council agreed that Jesus deserved to be put to death.

Jesus then faced abuse from those present. According to Luke, the abusers were "the men who were holding Jesus" (see Luke 22:63). Matthew wrote that these men spat in Jesus' face and hit him. Luke wrote that they also blindfolded him (see Luke 22:64). That fact explains Matthew's statement that they demanded that Jesus prophesy by telling them who had hit him. In this experience, Jesus fulfilled a prophecy of Isaiah: "I hid not my face from shame and spitting" (Isa. 50:6).

Peter's Denial (26:69-75)

Jesus was being tried inside the high priest's palace. But outside, Peter was undergoing a painful trial of his own.

As Peter sat in the high priest's courtyard, a servant girl approached him. She remarked that Peter had been with Jesus. Peter denied her statement to all who were in the courtyard with him, saying he didn't know what she meant. Surely a coward would have quickly left at that point. But Peter stayed on.

Later, on the porch, another servant girl told the bystanders that Peter had been with Jesus. This time Peter swore with an oath that he did not even know Jesus.

Still later, a bystander accused Peter of being a follower of Jesus, saying that Peter's Galilean accent betrayed him as such. With even greater intensity than before, Peter swore that he did not know Jesus.

At that moment, Peter heard the cock crow. Whether this was a literal cock or the blowing of a Roman bugle at 3:00 AM makes little difference (see discussion of 26:30-35). The sound caused Peter to remember Jesus' prediction of denial. Sorrow at his disloyalty overwhelmed Peter, and "he went out and wept bitterly" (v. 75).

Often we are harsh in judging Peter's disloyalty to Jesus at this time. But remember that the other disciples had all run away. Peter had cared enough and had courage enough to follow at a distance to see what would happen to Jesus.

If Peter had not had the courage to follow, he would not have had to face the situation in which he denied Jesus. However wrong Peter's denial was, he deserves credit for his courage and for the love which led him to the high priest's courtyard.

It seems certain that Peter himself told this story. Otherwise the New Testament Gospels would have no record of it. It might seem strange that Peter would ever tell others this story in which he appeared so weak. But in light of later events, Peter could say that Jesus had forgiven him and reclaimed him in spite of the weakness he had shown in denying him.

To Pilate (27:1-2)

Early the next morning, the Sanhedrin met again, this time officially and legally. The meeting seems to have been for the purpose of deciding what charge to bring against Jesus so that the Romans would put him to death.

At this time the Sanhedrin lacked the power to put a person to death (see John 18:31). But Rome would never execute a person on a charge of blasphemy. That charge had to do only with the Jewish law.

Matthew has not given us an account of the council's proceedings. But evidently the members of the Sanhedrin decided to accuse Jesus of treason. After all, the Romans considered anyone who claimed messiahship a dangerous revolutionary. Their scheming done, the Sanhedrin had Jesus bound and sent to Pontius Pilate, the Roman governor of Judea.

Judas' Tragic End (27:3-10)

Realizing that Jesus had been condemned, Judas "repented" (v. 3) of his act of betrayal. Had he really expected that the arrest would prompt Jesus to lead a revolt against Rome? We have no way of knowing the reasons for Judas' remorse.

Judas did, however, return the thirty silver shekels to the elders and chief priests. He confessed to them that Jesus was innocent, and that in betraying Jesus, he had sinned.

But the religious authorities had only contempt for Judas. They had used him for their own purposes and were now finished with him. They would not reconsider their action against Jesus.

In despair, Judas threw down the money in the Temple. Then, seeing no relief for his guilt, he committed suicide by hanging himself. Notice that he had repented only to the religious leaders. He had not asked forgiveness from God, and so his guilt was more than he could bear.

The chief priests had been glad enough to pay Judas for betraying Jesus. They had had no qualms at all about sending the innocent Jesus to his death. But they decided that to put the thirty shekels in the Temple treasury would be unlawful. After all, the money was "blood money" (v. 6).

They finally agreed to use the money to buy a field for the burial of "strangers," (v. 7) who might die while in Jerusalem. Matthew saw this act as fulfilling Old Testament Scripture (see Jer. 32:7-9 and Zech. 11:12-13).

Jesus Before Pilate (27:11-26)

Questions from Pilate (27:11-14).—Pilate, the Roman governor of Judea, was in Jerusalem at this time, though his official residence was in Caesarea. The governor first asked Jesus if it were true that he was King of the Jews" (v. 11). It would seem that the religious authorities had charged that Jesus had claimed this title.

Jesus' answer, "You have said so," (v. 11) was an affirmative one. But it implied that Jesus understood the title in a way far different from the way Pilate understood it.

Next, the elders and chief priests hurled their accusations at Jesus. Jesus refused to reply to their charges, knowing that their minds were already set against him. Pilate was surprised that Jesus made no reply to the authorities' charges. He asked Jesus, "Do you not hear how many things they testify against you?" (v. 13). But Jesus did not answer Pilate's question either. In this instance, the prophecy found in Isaiah 53:7 was fulfilled, for though "oppressed," and "afflicted," Jesus "opened not his mouth."

Jesus or Barabbas (27:15-23).—Evidently Pilate saw no reason to believe that Jesus was guilty of treason. At Passover, it was customary for the governor to release a prisoner for the people. Pilate took advantage of this custom to try to win the crowd's approval for Jesus' release. A man named Barabbas was being held in prison. This man had been imprisoned for murder and insurrection (see Luke 23:19). Pilate offered to release either Jesus or Barabbas for the crowd. He must have thought they would ask for Jesus' release.

Meanwhile, a message came to Pilate from his wife. Of all the Gospel writers, only Matthew included this story. Pilate's wife warned her husband to "Have nothing to do with" the righteous Jesus (v. 19). A dream about him had disturbed her greatly.

The elders and the chief priests, however, stirred up the crowd against Jesus. They persuaded the people to call for Barabbas' release instead of Jesus'. When the crowd's verdict was in, Pilate asked them what he should then do about Jesus. Perhaps he hoped they would ask for a lighter punishment than crucifixion. But, urged on by the authorities, the people cried out for Jesus' death by crucifixion.

Pilate's decision (27:24-26).—Pilate found himself in a difficult situation. He saw the beginnings of a riot which could become serious if he went ahead and released Jesus. It was highly important that he keep the peace in Jerusalem if he wanted to retain his position. And he needed the support of the religious authorities, who were urging Jesus' crucifixion. Yet Pilate must have seen the sentencing of an innocent man to death as a betrayal of Roman justice.

Pilate literally "washed his hands" (v. 24) of the matter, using this Jewish custom to proclaim his innocence (see Deut. 21:6-7). He declared himself innocent of Jesus' blood and put the blame on the people. The people gladly accepted for themselves and their children the responsibility for the shedding of Jesus' blood.

Then Pilate set Barabbas free. Interestingly enough, some ancient manuscripts tell us that Barabbas' first name was also Jesus. Jesus means Savior. The people had two saviors to choose between. They chose the one who wanted to save them from Rome rather than the one who had come to save them from sin. Jesus was executed for the crime of which Barabbas was actually guilty.

Pilate had Jesus scourged in preparation for execution. Scourging was a severe beating with a whip made from strips of leather weighted with bits of bone or metal. Some prisoners died from scourging. When this terrible beating was finished, Pilate delivered Jesus up for crucifixion.

Mocking by Roman Soldiers (27:27-31)

Pilate's soldiers then took Jesus into the governor's palace. Already badly beaten, Jesus now had to face more mocking and ridicule.

Because of the charge against Jesus, and probably also because of his unkingly appearance, the soldiers stripped his own clothing off him and dressed him in the mock array of a king. They put a scarlet robe, probably belonging to a Roman soldier, on him. On his head they placed a crown woven out of thorns. In his right hand they placed a reed representing a king's scepter.

Then the soldiers knelt before Jesus, calling out in ridicule, "Hail, King of the Jews!" (v. 29). With contempt, they spat in Jesus' face and hit his head with the reed.

Their cruel game over, the soldiers put Jesus' own clothes back on him. Then they led him toward the place where he would face execution. In that day, crucifixions occurred frequently, and carrying them out was part of the Roman soldiers' work. They could have had no idea that Jesus' crucifixion would be any different from any which had gone before.

The Scene at Golgotha (27:32-44)

Crucifixion was the form of execution the Romans used for slaves, the very worst criminals, and rebels. Jesus was to be executed on the false charge of being a rebel, a traitor against Rome.

By custom, the condemned man carried the horizontal crossbeam (not the whole cross in most cases) to the place of execution. However, a passerby, Simon of Cyrene, was conscripted to carry Jesus' crossbeam. Evidently the scourging and long night of hearings had already weakened Jesus' body considerably.

The place of Jesus' crucifixion was called Golgotha, "the place of a skull" (v. 33). It seems to have been a hill with a shape like a skull. There Jesus was crucified (his hands and feet nailed to the cross) between two robbers who may have been followers of Barabbas (see 27:16-17). Over Jesus' head was placed a placard reading, "This is Jesus the King of the Jews" (v. 37). This inscription announced the crime of which Jesus was accused. It must also have been a Roman jibe at the religious leaders.

Jesus refused the painkilling drink he was offered. He wanted to face his ordeal with a clear and fully conscious mind. He refused to avoid the pain as well. Beneath him, the Roman soldiers kept watch to prevent Jesus' followers from taking him from the cross before he died. These pagan soldiers followed the usual custom of casting lots for Jesus' clothing. But in doing so, they fulfilled Psalm 22:18.

While on the cross, in the midst of the greatest physical agony, Jesus faced ridicule from three different groups.

Passersby brought up the distorted version of his saying about destroying the Temple and rebuilding it in three days (see discussion of 26:57-68). They mockingly challenged him to save himself by getting down from the cross. Their words "If you are the Son of God . . . " (v. 40) were reminiscent of those of Satan during Jesus' wilderness temptations (see 4:3,6). Even on the cross Jesus faced temptation. Of course, if Jesus had saved himself at this point, he could not have gone on to save others.

The religious leaders (the elders, scribes, and chief priests) also came to the cross to ridicule Jesus. They thought they had finally won their battle against him. These also scornfully challenged him to save himself, saying they would believe in him if he could perform that mighty work of self-rescue. They taunted him with his claim of being God's Son, saying that surely God would save one who so greatly trusted in him, unless God, too, had rejected Jesus.

Even the robbers on Jesus' right and left "reviled him in the same way" (v. 44). Luke, however, wrote that one of them became a believer before he died (see Luke 23:39-43).

The Death of Jesus (27:45-50)

From noon until three o'clock in the afternoon, the land was covered in darkness. Perhaps this darkness was symbolic of God's judgment upon those who had rejected his Son. It isn't surprising that nature reacted with darkness during the hours when the Creator hung dying on the cross.

About three o'clock, Jesus cried out with the words of Psalm 22:1, "My God, my God, why hast thou forsaken me?" (v. 46). All the words of that Psalm must have been in Jesus' mind as the events surrounding his death unfolded. Psalm 22 contains the words of one who felt separated from God as he suffered alone. Yet the ending of the psalm was one of triumphant faith. Notice that even in the midst of his pain and suffering, Jesus could still call his Father "My God" (v. 46). God the Father was there in this whole event, using it to reconcile the world to himself. But Jesus was bearing the sin of the world. The one who had been totally free from sin was now bearing the world's sin.

This cry of Jesus is the only one of Jesus' sayings from the cross preserved by Matthew and Mark. Others can be found in Luke's and John's Gospels.

Some of those who stood by the cross heard Jesus' cry and misunderstood it. They thought that in his distress, he was calling out to Elijah for help. (It was believed that Elijah came to rescue righteous Jews when they were in need.) One, perhaps a soldier, offered Jesus some sour wine for his thirst. Others wanted to wait and see whether Elijah would come to rescue Jesus from the cross.

Then, after a loud cry, Jesus "yielded up his spirit" (v. 50). That loud cry may have been the words recorded by Luke, "Father, into thy hands I commit my spirit!" (Luke 23:46). Or, it may be that his cry consisted of those words preserved by John, "It is finished" (John 19:30).

Often those who were crucified lived for days. Jesus died after only a few hours. Both physical weakness from scourging and the tremendous spiritual load he bore must have been factors in his quick death. The wording used by Matthew here (v. 50) shows that Jesus' life was not taken from him. He voluntarily gave it up.

People and Events Surrounding the Crucifixion (27:51-56)

Two spectacular events accompanied Jesus' death. First, the veil at the entrance of the Temple's Holy of Holies (which the high priest alone could enter) was torn in two from top to bottom, possibly by an earthquake. There are two possible interpretations of the rending of the veil. It is likely that both are applicable. God's judgment for Israel's unbelief is one interpretation. The other is the opening to all people of direct access to God because of Jesus' death.

The earthquake split rocks and caused tombs to open. Matthew wrote that later, after Jesus had been raised from the dead, the bodies of many of God's people buried near Jerusalem were raised. These were even seen in Jerusalem itself. This event symbolized Jesus' conquering of death.

The earthquake was awe-inspiring to the centurion on duty and those serving under him. They declared that Jesus must have been God's Son after all. We cannot know how much they meant by their statement. They could have been saying only that Jesus was a hero who must be divine. Or, they may have sensed that Jesus' claims about himself must be true.

Matthew listed witnesses to the events surrounding Jesus' crucifixion. These were women who were among Jesus' Galilean followers. They had followed Jesus to Jerusalem to minister to him. Matthew named several who watched from a distance as Jesus died on the cross: Mary Magdalene; another Mary who was "the mother of James and Joseph"; and the mother of James and John, the Sons of Zebedee (v. 56). No doubt Matthew felt these women deserved credit for their faithfulness in being there during the time of Jesus' greatest trial and suffering.

Burial in Joseph's Tomb (27:57-61)

The Jewish law required that the body of an executed man be buried the same day death occurred (see Deut. 21:22-23). Jesus died

about three o'clock on Friday afternoon. It was necessary then that
he be buried before the Sabbath began at sunset.

Joseph of Arimathea, called "a rich man" (v. 57) by Matthew,
asked and received permission from Pilate to take the body of Jesus
and give it burial. Who was Joseph? Matthew wrote that Joseph
"was a disciple of Jesus" (v. 57). John, in his Gospel, added that out
of fear of the Jewish authorities, Joseph's discipleship was secret
(John 19:38). Mark and Luke both noted that Joseph was actually a
member of the Sanhedrin, the council which had decided to have
Jesus put to death (Mark 15:43; Luke 23:50). Luke wrote that Joseph
"had not consented" to the council's "purpose and deed" (Luke
23:51).

Risking disapproval from his fellow council members, Joseph followed the Jewish custom of wrapping the body in a clean linen
shroud (27:59). He then placed Jesus' body in a new tomb he had
had prepared for himself.

This tomb was hewn out of rock and had a large, probably circu-
lar stone for sealing the entrance. Joseph left after he had rolled the
stone over the entrance. (See John 19:39-40 for additional details
about Jesus' burial.)

At least two of Jesus' women followers from Galilee watched as
Joseph laid Jesus' body in the tomb. These were two of the women
who had seen the crucifixion from a distance, "Mary Magdalene and
the other Mary" (v. 61).

The Guard (27:62-66)

Only Matthew has left a record of an action taken by the Jewish
authorities after Jesus' death. On the sabbath, the day after Jesus
had died, the Pharisees and chief priests went to Pilate to make a
request. They told Pilate that Jesus had promised to rise from the
dead three days after his death. They feared that Jesus' disciples
would steal their Master's body and then claim that he had risen.
That fraud, they declared, would be even worse than Jesus' fraudu-
lent claim to be the Messiah.

They asked, then, that Pilate make the tomb secure until Jesus had
been dead three days. The Jews believed that death was irrevocable
after a person had been dead three days, since by then the spirit had
left the body.

Pilate agreed to the religious leaders' request. He gave them a group of soldiers to guard the tomb, and the stone at the tomb's entrance was sealed.

News of the Resurrection (28:1-7)

Early on Sunday morning, Mary Magdalene and Mary the mother of James and Joseph went back to Jesus' tomb. According to Mark's and Luke's Gospels, they were bringing spices to anoint Jesus' body (see Mark 16:1; Luke 24:1).

The women were greeted by a sight very different from anything they had expected. Either just before or at the time of their arrival at the tomb, "there was a great earthquake" (v. 2). An angel came down out of heaven, rolled the stone away from the stone's entrance and, in triumph, sat on the stone.

The angel's dazzling appearance was a shock to the Roman guards, who trembled and fell unconscious. The two Marys must have also been astonished. But the angel gave them a message of comfort. Jesus, he told them, had risen from the dead, as he had predicted. His former burial place was now empty, and they could easily verify this fact for themselves. His resurrection had been a bodily one.

The angel then sent the women on a mission. They were to find Jesus' disciples and tell them the wonderful news of the resurrection. They were also to tell the disciples that Jesus would precede them to Galilee. When they returned to Galilee, they would find him there already.

We know from accounts in the other Gospels that in addition to appearances in Galilee, Jesus also appeared to his disciples while they were still in Jerusalem. However, for Matthew, the most important of Jesus' appearances took place in Galilee.

A Meeting With Jesus (28:8-10)

The women quickly left the tomb to carry out the angel's instructions. Fear mingled with the joy they felt as they ran to tell the eleven remaining disciples the news of the resurrection.

As they went, Jesus himself met them. This meeting was not merely a vision. The women were able to grasp his feet in an act of worship. He was the Jesus they remembered. But now they recognized him as deserving the worship belonging to God alone.

Jesus repeated the instructions the angel had given the women (see 28:7). There was one important change, however. He called his disciples "my brethren" (v. 10). They had failed him completely in his time of greatest trial. But Jesus forgave them and looked ahead to what they would be as they served him in the future.

A Cover-up of the Truth (28:11-15)

While the two Marys were on their way to tell the disciples the good news, some of the Roman soldiers who had been guarding Jesus' tomb also went into Jerusalem. There they truthfully told the chief priests about the supernatural events which had occurred.

After a meeting with the elders, the chief priests decided that their best course of action would be to bribe the soldiers to cover up the truth. The soldiers accepted payment and agreed to say that they had fallen asleep while on guard, and Jesus' disciples had meanwhile stolen the body. The religious authorities told the soldiers that they would see that no punishment came to them if Pilate heard the story.

Only Matthew, of the four Gospel writers, has told us how the religious authorities answered the fact of the empty tomb. No one denied that the tomb was empty and that Jesus' body could not be found. Matthew declared that even when he was writing his Gospel, this false explanation was still being circulated to keep people from believing in the resurrection.

A Worldwide Mission (28:16-20)

Jesus' eleven remaining disciples followed his instruction to return to Galilee. We do not know exactly when Jesus' appearance recorded in verses 16-20 came in relation to his appearances recorded by Luke and John.

Matthew wrote that Jesus met the disciples at a prearranged site, a mountain. In the Old Testament as well as in Jesus' ministry, a mountain was often the place of divine revelation. Jesus had given his great sermon on a mountain. And he had been transfigured on another mountain. Now, also on a mountain, Jesus was going to commission his disciples for their task of taking his gospel to the world.

According to Matthew, the disciples worshiped Jesus, though

some of them experienced doubt. This fact may be explained by the theory of some Bible scholars that the eleven were not the only followers of Jesus present at the mountain that day. These interpreters see this appearance of Jesus as being the one Paul wrote about in 1 Corinthians 15:6, an appearance to five hundred of his followers at one time. Of course, it is possible that some of the eleven still had doubts about the amazing things which had happened.

Jesus announced to the disciples that he had been given "All authority in heaven and on earth" (v. 18). What an amazing statement! Jesus had accepted earthly limitations when he came to save the people of earth. But now, in his glorified, resurrected body, all authority was his.

Because Jesus possessed that authority, he could instruct his disciples to make all the world's nations his disciples. Baptism, the sign that a person has entered into God's possession, was to be done "in the name of the Father and of the Son and of the Holy Spirit" (v. 19).

The new disciples were to be taught as Jesus had taught his first disciples. But the emphasis was to be on the living out of the teachings.

Jesus closed his commission with the greatest of all promises. He would not be simply a fond memory to the disciples. Instead, he would always be present with them as they carried out his mission to the world. He would, in fact, be with them "to the close of the age" (v. 20), until God had accomplished his purpose for the world, and earth's history had come to an end.

Bibliography

General Works

Bauman, Edward W. *The Life and Teachings of Jesus.* Grand Rapids: Zondervan Publishing House, 1972.

Guthrie, Donald. *New Testament Introduction.* London: The Tyndale Press, 1970.

Guthrie, Donald. *Jesus the Messiah.* Grand Rapids: Zondervan Publishing House, 1972.

Hunter, Archibald M. *The Work and Words of Jesus.* London: SCM Press LTD, 1950.

Price, James L. *Interpreting the New Testament.* New York: Holt, Rinehart and Winston, 1961.

Throckmorton, Burton H., Jr., Ed. *Gospel Parallels.* New York: Thomas Nelson and Sons, 1957.

Commentaries

Allen, Clifton J., Ed. *The Broadman Bible Commentary,* Vol. 8. Nashville: Broadman Press, 1969.

Barclay, William. *The Daily Study Bible,* Vols. 1,2. *The Gospel of Matthew.* Philadelphia: The Westminster Press, 1956.

Barclay, William. *The Old Law and the New Law.* Philadelphia: The Westminster Press, 1972.

Buttrick, George, Ed. *The Interpreter's Bible,* Vol. 7. New York: Abingdon Press, 1951.

Dietrich, Suzanne de. *The Layman's Bible Commentary, The Gospel According to Matthew,* Vol. 16. Atlanta: John Knox Press, 1961.

Eiselen, Frederick C., Ed. *The Abingdon Bible Commentary.* New York: Abingdon Press, 1929.

Hobbs, Herschel H. *An Exposition of the Gospel of Matthew.* Grand Rapids: Baker Book House, 1965.

Hunter, Archibald M. *Interpreting the Parables.* Philadelphia: The Westminster Press, 1960.

Robertson, A. T. *Word Pictures in the New Testament,* Vol. 1. Nashville: Broadman Press, 1930.

Tasker, R. V. G. *Tyndale New Testament Commentaries, The Gospel According to St. Matthew,* Vol. 1. Grand Rapids: William B. Eerdmans Publishing Co., 1961.

Tolbert, Malcolm O. *Good News from Matthew.* Nashville: Broadman Press, 1975.